LIBERTY UNIVERSITY
JOHN W. RAWLINGS SCHOOL OF DIVINITY

A CHRISTIAN PERSPECTIVE ON ISLAM'S ORIGINS

Its Religion, Founder, and Practices

Apologetic Thesis

by

GABRIEL ARYEH

July 25, 2022

ISBN 979-8-88943-824-3 (paperback)
ISBN 979-8-88943-825-0 (digital)

Christian Faith Publishing
832 Park Avenue
Meadville, PA 16335
www.christianfaithpublishing.com

Printed in the United States of America

Contents

Introduction

Many years ago, during this writer's adolescent and teen years growing up in the Bronx, New York, Islam's presence throughout New York City's five boroughs seemed an oddity in some of these areas but a grave challenge in other neighborhoods to the Christians living close to specific madrasas (e.g., Brooklyn and Queens Islamic schools). The Islamic religion and practices appeared somewhat confusing, concerning how many of its adherents acted upon them and demonstrated their faith in the prophet Muhammad and his deity Allah. Each Muslim group enacted its beliefs slightly differently from the other. Like Christian denominational distinctions on doctrines affecting quotidian life and practices structured on biblical texts and traditions without deviating from core theological truths forming "nonnegotiable" dogma, major Islamic groups and their smaller sects maintain a similar pattern of central beliefs. However, despite impressive hermeneutic investigations showing a Syriac-Aramaic literary influence in the sacred Islamic Arabic texts and the archaeological discoveries of many modern scholars to establish Islam's connections to its monotheistic Abrahamic predecessors, this author argues that Islam identifies as a paganized Judeo-Christian cult. Thus, this student's thesis will delve into the origins of the Islamic religion and its practices that form the core beliefs of the principal sects and smaller movements of the Muslims, which appear normative and immutable tenets followed by all its adherents worldwide.

The task mentioned above will commence by briefly investigating the ancient Arab peoples' initial appearance, migrations, and theistic beliefs to understand the rise of Muhammad's prophethood, religious theology, and political unification message to the Arabic peoples, which formed Islam's current spiritual state. Hence, by briefly showing the Islamic religion's emergence, it will become easier for Christians (and secular Westerners) to understand the typical behavioral patterns associated with Islam's current theological claims and attitudes toward all unbelievers.

The questions about Islam that usually stir the interest of curious Western academics and civilians working among fellow citizens adhering to the Islamic faith surround the authenticity of its religious claims suggesting its Abrahamic lineage and relationship to its forerunners, Judaism and Christianity. After all, monotheism in the religious study became associated mainly with the Abrahamic faith professed by the ancient Jewish people and the Hellenistic Jews, whom many became Christians when they correlated Messianic prophetic fulfillments with *Yeshua*, the son of Mary, and recognized him as God Himself. This author's observation appears credible despite other religious and historical claims, which seem more of an opinion than factual.

For example, Yamauchi dispels the claim that Ahura Mazda (Ormazd, the Zoroastrian deity) influenced Jewish monotheism and eschatology. Ormazd worshipped Mithra in legends of the ninth century AD. Thus, framing Zoroastrianism as the first monotheistic religion is fallacious, considering that Angra Mainyu (deity of evil) coexisted with Ahura Mazda in conflict throughout millennia per earlier dates.[1] However, amalgamating Islam with Judaism and Christianity at a theological level will prove problematic as one delves deeper into the Islamic deific origins of Allah, acknowledged by all Muslim believers and many Western Christian academics.

Moreover, the actions described by Muhammad, the founder and designer of the Islamic faith, place an additional vexation on the legitimacy of its Abrahamic lineage and tradition when it depicts a form of revelation foreign to the stylistic reception known by the

---

[1] Daniel I. Block, *Israel: Ancient Kingdom or Late Invention?* (Nashville, TN. B&H Academic, 2008), 282–97. Block highlights and affirms the uniqueness of Yahwist monotheism among the Ancient Near Eastern nations. Daniel Block, *The Gods of the Nations: A Study in Ancient Near Eastern National Theology. 2nd Ed.* (Eugene, OR: Wipf and Stock Publishers, 2000), 58, 63–6, 68–9, 72, 150.

Jewish prophets and writers. Finally, these observations in the two statements above place a theological strain on the claims of Islam's Abrahamic origins as one observes the current religious practices in the areas exercised and recognized as "*halal*" (Arabic word for *permissible*), contradicting Judaic and Christian theologies. Thus, Islam's origins contain biographical and revelatory receptive patterns refuting its alleged theological continuation of Judaism or Christianity, which ultimately claims itself the seal of the Abrahamic faiths. This researcher will undoubtedly show its unwarranted, fallacious legitimacy proclaimed by numerous Western scholars. Although Western academics consistently attempt to nobly extend an olive branch to Islam by including them into the Abrahamic monotheistic tradition by providing academic volumes of information based on modern scholarly commentaries, they fail to present evidence from authentic Islamic sources to prove their theological positions. Therefore, this writer will introduce original Islamic sources like hadith collections, tafsirs, and Qur'anic texts to contrast their historical, geographical, and theological content with other religious and secular sources that maintain massive historic documentation pointing to Islam's development.

The Ancient Arabs

In the modern West, when most think about the Arab culture spreading throughout the Middle Eastern countries, it usually relates in one way or another to the dominance of the Islamic presence in its governmental structures, religious ideologies, or military strength influencing the Middle East. Moreover, Western societies tend to associate the Arabic culture as entirely defined by the religion of Islam because most people, but more specifically, academics, claim how Islamic ingenuity completely dominated large swaths of what was identified as the previous mighty Byzantine and Persian Empires. Still, through Islam's "magnificent" military and political conquests initiated through its religious ideologies, the Arabic people became synonymous with historical Islamic exploits and cultural influences, integrated with most Middle Eastern nations worldwide.[2]

However, the historical connection between Arabic culture and Islam has not always existed by association. The Arab peoples operated under slightly different ideas than the Islamic ideals espoused by its supposed founder, Muhammad, who greatly influenced his religious beliefs and lifestyle during his alleged prophetic ministry. Islam's successive expansions lie in Muhammad's early military exploits and the ingenuity of its prior immigrants and conquered peoples whose previous experience of living in societies ethically, politically, and scientifically superior to the Meccan Arabs advanced the Muslim world. Thus, we can immediately begin this investigation by dispelling all

---

[2] For example, this author believes after a massive amount of research that despite Islam's illustrious conquests initially coming from Arabic governance, much is owed to the integration of the Persian rulers, the Seljuk, and Ottoman Turks, by which Islam spread much more than in the Arab era of expansion.

mythical claims made by many Western academics who rave about the alleged "golden ages" in Iraq and Spain and other intellectual leaps brought by the "brilliance" and "tolerance" of Arabic Islamic culture.[3] Most early Muslim caliphates, like Muawiya I and II, brutally attacked the Iraqi and Assyrian Christians. They later assaulted the Byzantines at Rhodes, destroying any pre-Islamic work of art or religious artifact considered from a Jahiliya period, suggesting the Islamic ignorance of any land before Islam's conquest.[4] Moreover, conquerors like Tariq and the Umayyad caliph Umar ibn Abd al-Aziz enslaved the Spanish, and enslaving their women was on the top of their list of "things to do," affirming that their cruelties sanctioned by their Islamic theologies proved the golden ages are a farce.[5] On a side note, Spencer shows that from the time of Tariq (711 AD) through the following seven hundred years, Spain continued fighting the Muslim invaders, affirming the statement above regarding the "golden years."[6]

Still, before the rise of Islam, the pride of the Arabic peoples came from their prowess in combat, their ability to maintain themselves as a center of trade for millennia while keeping foreigners away from their sources, and their infamous caravan raids. Gibson points

---

[3] One can use a primary example provided by Fernandez-Morera, who rightly points out some of the fallacious writings of various Western scholars like Breiner, Troll, and Appiah extolling and falsely attributing philosophical, scientific, and societal contributions to the Muslims under the alleged tolerance of their Islamic rule in Iraq and Spain. Dario Fernandez-Morera, *The Myth of the Andalusian Paradise: Muslims, Christians, and Jews Under Islamic Rule in Medieval Spain* (Wilmington, DE: ISI Books, 2016), 1–2, 5–7, 10, 12–3, 48–9. Goldschmidt and Boum briefly mention the alleged golden age of Baghdad (Iraq), allegedly brought under the Abbasid caliphate from the ninth to tenth century AD. Arthur Goldschmidt Jr. and Aomar Boum, *A Concise History of the Middle East. 11th Ed* (Boulder, CO: Westview Press, 2016), 66, 73.

[4] Spencer shows that these events occurred during the seventh and eighth centuries AD. Moreover, the Spanish continued to fight the Islamic occupations of their lands until they finally freed themselves from their grasp. Robert Spencer, *The History of Jihad from Muhammad to Isis* (New York, NY: Bombardier Books, 2018), 66, 74–5, 79–80, 83.

[5] Ibid.

[6] Ibid.

out how the Arab traders suppressed information from the Romans concerning their sources of frankincense and other goods by creating myths.[7] During pre-Islamic times, Arabic poetry centered on the bravery of its tribal warriors, honor, and strengths as they raided their neighboring tribes and foreigners that traded throughout the Arabian Peninsula (AP).[8] Moreover, the Arabic peoples survived the harsh climate by domesticating camels for commercial and quotidian usage, living as nomads, and consistently moving around searching for water.

Geographic and Ethnic Origins

The Arabic peoples' geographic origins, genealogy, and theistic beliefs pervading their various ethnic and religious groups significantly influenced the Islamic founder's faith. Supposedly, Muhammad initiated, established, and categorized ritualistic practices as required acts of Muslim worship according to some of the prevalent socioreligious beliefs of the Arabic peoples. One must recognize the importance of identifying the Arabic culture through its origins because it ultimately points to the genealogy initiating their emergence. Secondly, we must understand the Arabic people's role in Muhammad's religious appeal for deific authentication as a prophet to the Bedouin Arabs. Still, the Quraysh tribe will help us understand the significance of why he alluded to their prime deity, Allah.

Oddly, the first part of this investigation mentioned above becomes challenging if one solely relies on secular sources of history because they do not offer a solid genealogical record capable of solving the Arab's mysterious origins, significant to Muhammad's claims of prophetic authenticity. For example, Macintosh-Smith rightly points out that Arab refers to a mobile minority or nomadic group. Hence, the word *Arab* becomes definitionally equivalent to the initial use of

---

[7]   Dan Gibson, *The Nabataeans: Builders of Petra* (Orlando, FL: Xlibris, 2022), 81–3, 161–3.
   Ibid., Goldschmidt and Boum, 19–20.

[8]   Tim Macintosh-Smith, *Arabs: A 3,000-Year History of Peoples, Tribes, and Empires* (New Haven, CT: Yale University Press, 2019), 59, 61.

the term *pagan*, which meant "country dweller," despite being associated with the idolatrous connotations we immediately conjure up in modern Western thought. Hence, depicting a desert dweller does not lead to uncovering the Arabic ethnic origin. By Macintosh-Smith directly referring to alleged "mythical" tribes known in the Arab culture as "Ad" and "Thamud," he affirms this researcher's point made earlier.[9] This researcher highlights the previous observation because tracing the Arabic origins to tribal groups alone without mentioning these tribes' progenitors appears to be the best option most secular sources offer by not providing clear forebearers.

In contrast, the Arabic people's genealogical origins appear better represented by the biblical narrative than any other literature written by most secular or Islamic sources.[10] It traces its beginnings to specific personalities well-known to most Jewish and Christian scholars. According to the Bible, Central Arabic origins lie in the lineage of Keturah, the wife of Abraham, which this writer will present in the following sections under the themes addressing Muhammad's identity.[11] Keturah's children migrated to the land of the East, considered North Arabia, which points to the Arabic genealogy of the Central Arabs from whom the Meccans would technically trace their descent. The significance of mentioning the "East," from where Keturah's children migrated, is that this biblical fact corroborates most sources specifying the first historical mentions of their existence as the *Aribi*.[12]

---

[9] Tim Macintosh-Smith, *Arabs*, 27, 29.

[10] Dakdok shares this author's view (see 136). Usama K. Dakdok, *Exposing the Truth about the Qur'an: The Revelation of Error. The Stories of the Prophets. Vol. 1 of 2* (Venice, FL: Usama Dakdok Publishing, 2013), 135–6.

[11] Lockman Foundation, *Life Application Bible Study Bible. NASB. Genesis. 25:1–6* (Grand Rapids, MI: Zondervan, 2000), 52. J. I. Packer et al. *Enciclopedia Ilustrada de Realidades de la Biblia: Una Completa Fuente de Datos Sobre Personas, Lugares, y Costumbres de la Biblia. [Original title: Nelson's Illustrated Encyclopedia of Bible Facts. Thomas Nelson Publishers, 1980]* (Miami, FL: Caribe, 2002), 759.

[12] For example, the Eastern patriarch Job lived in the land of Uz. Ibid., Job. 1:1, 836.

According to Macintosh-Smith, ancient peoples traveled into the AP from the Fertile Crescent and the Levant.[13] The significance of Macintosh-Smith's investigative conclusion is that it indirectly affirms the Bible's genealogical data by using Assyrian and Hebraic sources, which mention the Arabic peoples simultaneously. Thus, the hazy recognition of the Arabic peoples by secular and theistically oriented historical authorities affirms biblical genealogical claims concerning their original heritage.[14] Therefore, another part of this journey into the origins of Islam briefly looks at the AP itself, which in pre-Islamic times did not offer enough life-sustaining natural resources for people to live comfortably outside its border to the Fertile Crescent's southern side.[15]

The AP's geographical landscapes remained commercially valuable to ancient royalty (e.g., the northwestern side of the AP considered Arabia Petraea) as observed in the royal house of the Nabataeans, Petra, serving as convenient trade routes for exchanging and exporting the desert's unique products, which included tribal participation in the market.[16] During the slow declines of the Roman and Byzantine Empires, many religious dissidents sought refuge in the Persian kingdoms among its people. Its sporadic alliances with the Bedouin Arabs exposed the populace in the AP to Jewish monotheism and Christian sects fleeing religious persecution.[17] However, the Christianized Roman Empire had no genuine military desire to authorize the pursuit of any sectarian individuals or groups for reli-

---

[13] Macintosh-Smith mentions that the earliest reference to Arabs comes from the letters of the Assyrian king Shalmaneser III who mentions his altercation with the *"Aribi"* led by their leader Gindibu who supported a Syrian-Palestinian coalition. Tim Macintosh-Smith, *Arabs,* 30–2.

[14] Ibid., 30–1. Hatoon Ajwad al-Fassi, *Women in Pre-Islamic Arabia: Nabataea.* (Oxford, UK: Bar Publishing, 2016), 20. Usama K. Dakdok, *Exposing the Truth about the Qur'an. Vol. 1 of 2,* 135–6.

[15] Macintosh-Smith, *Arabs,* 22–3.

[16] For example, although much of the Arabian Peninsula stood as a desert environment, it produced trees and other costly materials that sold considerably well throughout the ancient world. Ibid., 23. Hatoon Ajwad al-Fassi, *Women in Pre-Islamic Arabia: Nabataea,* 29.

[17] Goldschmidt and Boum, *A Concise History of the Middle East,* 13–22.

gious reasons into the heart of the AP that could lead to an expensive mission against heretics or other theistic groups. Hence, the Roman Empire did not exercise its military strength against the inner parts of the AP because it held little significance regarding "religious" challenges before the arrival of the prophet Muhammad who later threatened the Byzantine and Persian Empires under Islam.[18]

Nevertheless, the information above about the Arabian Peninsula's diverse landscapes presents extreme difficulties for the Muslim narratives provided by the "canonical" Islamic sources because some of the geographical areas depicted contradict many of its historical affirmations. Ibn Ishaq describes the Mecca as a land filled with lush grass and trees despite no such depiction of the Meccan landscape in any historical source, whether pre-Islamic or otherwise.[19] Spencer points out that "Muhammad's Mecca" depicted in the hadith written by Bukhari did not resemble today's Meccan province or the seventh- and eighth-centuries' geography because it contained no mountainous areas.[20] Furthermore, the Islamic scholar Bukhari stated that Muhammad entered Mecca from the high Thaniya and left from its lower side, referring to a mountain.[21] However, Dan Gibson suggests that the geographical depictions above accurately fit the ancient and modern-day Petrean landscape instead of ancient or modern Mecca.[22] Hence, modern Muslims miserably fail to address the disturbing Meccan geography, countering their traditional narratives concerning its importance as an Arabian trade center.

Spencer highlights pre-Islamic historical sources like those of the Greek, Latin, and Indian chronicles by stating that they never mentioned Mecca as a vital trading center for spice or any other

---

[18] Ibid., 16.

[19] Alfred Guillaume, *The Life of Muhammad: A Translation of Ishaq's Sirat Rasul Allah* (Karachi, PAK: Oxford University Press, 2016), 38–9, 46, 52–4.

[20] Robert Spencer, *Did Muhammad Exist? An Inquiry into Islam's Obscure Origins. Revised and Expanded Edition* (New York, NY: Bombardier, 2021), 122–4.

[21] Muhammad, Khan. *The Translation of The Meanings of Sahih Al-Bukhari, Vol. 2, Book 25, Hadith 1575–80* (Riyadh, SAE: Darussalam, 2008), 374–5. Spencer, Did Muhammad Exist? 122–4.

[22] Spencer, *Did Muhammad Exist?* 122–4.

trade commodity because it remained relatively insignificant until the ninth century AD.[23] Moreover, the importance of Mecca's alleged role in the Arabic religious pilgrimages to the Kaaba appears doubtful considering the popularity of other similar religious structures used for worship in Petra, which seemed one of the highly favored places for pilgrimage.[24] For many years, this writer has believed that Petra (Arabia Petraea) is the birthplace of Islam due to its commercial importance in the ancient world, its geographical landscape resembling much of the hadith imagery cited above, and religious worship imitated by the initial and current Islamic rituals.

The author Michael Cook highlights the Qur'an's strange reference to Muhammad's "seafaring." Still, the *sira* of Muhammad never mentions any journey to the sea.[25] Moreover, Cook points out that the Qur'an clearly states Muhammad passes by the ruins of Sodom and Gomorrah every morning and night, suggesting he reflects on its destruction and shows that his Qureshi tribe's name, which means *shark*, remains an oddity concerning Mecca's location.[26] Thus, it seems that the ancestral progenitors of the modern-day Arabs lie in the Nabataeans, Sabeans, and previous Semitic peoples that populated the AP who brought their traditional trading methods and religious practices, which formed the Islamic religious and political character of the Muslim nations.[27] Therefore, the sections below will discuss the role of the Nabataean, Sabeans, Christian sectarians, and Judaic monotheistic beliefs that influenced the Islamic theistic origins, the alleged appearance of the Arabic prophet, and Islam's developmental process leading into its current religious form.

---

[23] Ibid., 114–7.

[24] Dan Gibson shows how most qiblas faced Petra instead of the insignificant Meccan province. Ibid., 117, 122.

[25] Ibn Warraq, *What the Koran Really Says: Language, Text, and Commentary* (Amherst, NY: Prometheus Books, 2002), 703–4.

[26] Ibid., 703. Usama Dakdok, *The Generous Qur'an: An Accurate English Translation. Surah. 37:133–8* (Venice, FL: Usama Dakdok, 2015), 261.

[27] Gibson outlines the origin of the Arabic peoples by tracing archaeological findings and literary evidence mentioning the Nabataeans, Sabeans, and other Semitic peoples. Gibson, *The Nabataeans,* 16–21, 111–9, 124.

Religious Cults in the Arab Peninsula

As we move further into the religious cults of the various regions in the Arabian Peninsula (AP), the origins of its people still form a large part of the conversation. Hence, one must attain a complete picture of Muhammad's world and the religious contributors propelling his prophethood to the Arabs proclaiming his Islamic belief. Thus, this thesis will present the peoples, practices, and rituals that formed the traditions identifying the Arabic culture before and during the days of Muhammad. Moreover, by giving the information above through ancient and modern Islamic, Jewish, Christian, and secular historical sources, this writer can begin building a compelling case in the later sections involving the reasoning behind Muhammad's rise and success in the religious unification of the AP. After all, Muhammad's fame as a prophet, military leader, and most excellent example of moral, spiritual, and societal conduct for all believing Muslims came from an appeal to his tribe's main deity Allah, who compels all believers to follow and obey by divine mandate.[28]

As stated earlier, this researcher believes that Islam's religious roots began in Arabia Petraea, where the illustrious Nabataeans resided centuries before and after the Muhammadan rise of Islamic rule over the entirety of the Arabian Peninsula. However, one should carefully consider the contributions of Semitic migrations into the AP, the Southern Arabian kingdoms, and the nomadic Bedouin Arabs, who had a trading relationship with the Nabataeans. Moreover, the lin-

---

[28] Dakdok, *The Generous Qur'an. Surah. 33:1–3*, 21, 241, 243.

guistic connections found within the peoples mentioned above show an overall integration that must have gradually taken place over the centuries leading to the religious conglomeration creating the unified "Arabic" movement that contributed significantly to the Islamic dominance of the Middle East. Undoubtedly, in conjunction with the Jewish and sectarian Christian refugees, the groups mentioned above brought many deities and ceremonial practices that formed Islam's exclusively Arabic monotheistic theology and proper techniques. The religious contributions of each group mentioned above clarify why Islam established Allah's worship by divine mandate in the following sections.

Nabataeans

In this writer's opinion, the most economically powerful and religiously influential of the ancient groups mentioned above related to the Meccan Arabs through a linguistic connection more than an ethnic one (further discussed in Muhammad's genealogy) are the Nabataeans. The Nabataean historical interactions with other Arabs of the AP, whether nomadic tribes or those established in the Southern kingdoms (e.g., Sabeans), tell us that they were not necessarily considered Arab despite their apparent linguistic connection.[29] Still, the Nabataean connection to the modern Arabs lies in the Arabic language, evident in their parental Aramaic script and Semitic origins.

Interestingly, Gibson highlights the Nabataean pantheon, which contained many deities that made their way into the Meccan province where Muhammad allegedly resided. However, for our purposes in this literary work, we will only focus on gods mentioned in the Islamic sources and additional deific names that will help shed light on the "Allah" of the ancient Arabic peoples predating Islam and how it influenced seventh-century Muslims to form their theology. The names of Allah, Al-Lat, Al-Uzza, and Manat in qur'anic literature

---

[29] Gibson, *The Nabataeans: Builders of Petra*, 18–21. Al-Fassi suggests that the Nabataeans originated from the Arabs, although historians remain uncertain if they identified themselves as Arabic like all the Arabian Peninsula (AP). Al-Fassi, *Women in Pre-Islamic Arabia: Nabataea*, 19–20.

remain significant to Islam's religious connections to the deities of the Nabataean pantheon.[30] Thus, merging deific attributes with the pagan gods mentioned above will clarify Allah's Muhammadan identity and its usefulness in unifying the AP's peoples under Islamic rule.

First, some of the Nabataean deities paralleled the deific figures that all Arabs of the AP worshiped for centuries and were exposed to through the established religious beliefs of the great Egyptian, Assyrian, Greek, and Roman Empires and the nomadic Arab tribes.[31] The trading interactions between the Nabataeans and the empirical powers mentioned above carried over many overlapping deities as these nations rose and declined in power and immigrated to the more religiously tolerant Nabataean environment. Still, the ancient gods of the Nabataeans included a pantheon, which contained deities such as Allah, Al-Lat, al-Uzza, and interestingly, the deity Dushara, who coincidentally identified as their primary god.[32] One of the most interesting facts about the deities above is that Allah and Dushara appear similar in authority as the primary gods of the Nabataeans, which creates the question of whether these deities morphed over centuries into the highest deity of the modern Muslims.[33] Additionally, Al-Fassi suggests that Dushara, the god of the Nabataeans, had a "monotheizing" effect on the worshipers, which allegedly appears consistent with the people of pre-Islamic Mecca.[34]

The statement above makes sense considering the "deific morphing" that occurred throughout the ancient world as cultures interacted. Due to evolving myths, some of their divine figures absorbed the attributes of an earlier pagan deity. Pinch explains this researcher's observation by showing how the Greek historian Herodotus

---

[30] Dakdok, *The Generous Qur'an. Surah. 53:19–23*, 304. Muhammad Taqi-ud-Din Al-Hilali and Muhammad Muhsin Khan, *Interpretations of The Meanings of The Noble Qur'an in The English Language: A Summarized Version of At-Tabari, Al-Qurtubi, and Ibn Kathir with Comments from Sahih Al-Bukhari. 2:219; 53:19–22. Vol. 1* (Riyadh, SAU: Darussalam, 1996), 54, 667.

[31] Al-Fassi, *Women in Pre-Islamic Arabia: Nabataea*, 21, 26–9. Dan Gibson, The Nabataeans, 168.

[32] Ibid., Gibson, 170–77.

[33] Ibid., 168, 174–6, 209–10, 213. Tim Macintosh-Smith, *Arabs*, 124.

[34] Hatoon Ajwad al-Fassi, *Women in Pre-Islamic Arabia: Nabataea*, 21.

Helicarnassus (484–420 BC) identified Grecian deities with those of the Egyptian gods based on the continuous written records kept by the Egyptian priests he encountered during his alleged visit to Egypt.[35] Additionally, Pinch eloquently outlines the morphosis of the feminine deity Isis over the centuries, making her the principal deity of various cultures in the ancient world by absorbing the divine attributes of many local and foreign deities.[36] Finally, Pinch and Carroll display many other ancient Near Eastern deities becoming primary gods in other nations (see footnotes 32–33, 35–36).[37] For example, Gibson shows that the Nabataean gods recognized by the Meccan Arabs as Al-Lat and Al-Uzza probably existed initially as one deity to the Nabataeans instead of two.[38] Moreover, the deific trinitarian version found in the Nabataean pantheon could have partially played a role in the initial Islamic reaction to Christianity's Triune God much later because they possibly preemptively made a theistically unfounded parallel to the pagan Arab trinities.[39]

Sabeans

Like the Nabataeans mentioned above, the Sabeans economically dominated the frankincense trade, among other costly exports, during the height of their power in the Arabian Peninsula. Moreover, their irrigation ingenuity in the ancient world seems to have facilitated their role and ability as traders throughout the early centuries BC. Macintosh-Smith states that the Sabeans were the most famous South Arabs who developed a prosperous civilization due to their constructive ingenuity proven by the archaeological discoveries sug-

---

[35] Geraldine Pinch, *Egyptian Mythology: A Guide to the Gods, Goddesses, and Traditions of Ancient Egypt* (New York, NY: Oxford University Press, 2004), 34, 40, 42–3, 108–9, 148, 151. Ironically, Isis absorbed the divine qualities of the Petrean Al-Uzza. Gibson, *The Nabataeans*, 172.

[36] Ibid.

[37] Michael P. Carroll, *The Cult of the Virgin Mary: Psychological Origins* (Princeton, NJ: Princeton University Press, 1986), 5–9, 32.

[38] Ibid., Gibson, 176.

[39] Ibid., 176–7.

gesting that they engineered the irrigation system empowered by the Marib Dam (sixth century BC).[40] Sabeans created a "mini-ecosystem" facilitating the economic growth for the other Southern societies of Arabia like the Minaeans, Qatabanian, and Himyaris.[41]

However, like the Nabataeans, the Sabeans did not consider themselves ethnically Arabic because Arabs were considered the nomadic peoples of the desert, and their linguistic expression slightly varied from their neighbors in the western, northern, and central parts of Arabia.[42] Thousands of inscriptions from the eighth and sixth centuries BC show that no specific Southern Arabian peoples ever referred to themselves as Arabs or felt an ethnic tie to "Arabism," as mentioned earlier, these groups probably migrated from further northeast of the Fertile Crescent and "Arab" referred to nomadic desert groups.[43] Still, the Sabean's previous economic prosperity had greatly diminished by Islam's emergence, and their role as traders faded significantly.[44]

However, the religion of the Sabeans seems somewhat muddled by the common usage of "Sabians" espoused in the Qur'an, which has caused some scholars to conflate the terms without making any distinctions between the ethnos and religious beliefs of the Sabean people.[45] By the time the prophet Muhammad rose to power to establish the Islamic religion (if not the Umayyad and Abbasids), the Sabians he referred to were not the ethnic Sabeans but a well-known religious sect evolving from the merging of Jewish, Christian, and Zoroastrian

---

[40] Macintosh-Smith, *Arabs*, 49–51.

[41] Ibid. Tony Maalouf, *Arabs in the Shadow of Israel: The Unfolding of God's Prophetic Plan for Ishmael's Line* (Grand Rapids, MI: Kregel Publications, 2003), 21.

[42] Macintosh-Smith points out that the Sabeans most likely migrated from the Fertile Crescent like other Semitic groups and acted as a somewhat homogenous group of Syriac-Palestinian origins. Macintosh-Smith, *Arabs*, 49.

[43] Peter Webb, *Imagining the Arabs: Arab Identity and the Rise of Islam* (Edinburgh, UK: Edinburgh University Press, 2016), 32–6.

[44] Mark, Joshua J., "Kingdom of Saba. Pg, 9." *World History Encyclopedia*. Last modified March 02, 2018. https://www.worldhistory.org/Kingdom_of_Saba/.

[45] For example, Robert Spencer references the Sabians to insinuate their religion and ethnicity simultaneously without explaining any distinctions. Spencer, *Did Muhammad Exist?* 212–3.

theologies. Thus, historically contextualizing the Sabean polytheistic beliefs, one can discern the difference between Muhammad's Sabian believers and the ethnic Sabeans. Torrey makes an astute observation of the Sabians of Muhammad's time that seems to identify them with a Judaeo-Christian sect who allegedly followed the teachings of John the Baptist regarding the ritual of baptism but did not recognize the deity of Jesus Christ. Moreover, Torrey mentions the influence of the Babylonian and Persian dualism on the Judaic cult, later reshaped by some followers of John the Baptist, which later became known as the *nasorayya* (Nazarenes).[46]

However, all ethnicities found in the Arabian Peninsula would later ascribe to the "Arab" and, ultimately, "Muslim" identity. Nevertheless, the Sabeans and all Southern Arabic peoples with the Sabian cult appear possible because ritual elements of practices like the worship of stars and fire found in the former existed in the latter religious group. Still, the polytheistic system of the Sabeans seems much more ancient than the Sabians with whom the Quraysh identified Muhammad as one of its religious adherents.[47] For example, Bukhari mentions a woman labeling Muhammad as the "Sabi" with a new religion when certain men came looking for him.[48] Moreover, when a man named Thumama accepted the religion of Islam, residents in Mecca called him a "Sabi" because he changed his belief to Muhammad's religious faith.[49] Still, what matters about the observa-

---

[46] Charles C. Torrey, A New Era in the History of the "Apocrypha." *The Monist* 25, no. 2 (1 April 1915), 286–294. https://doi.org/10.5840/monist191525211. Retrieved from Monist and Sabians Google Scholar.pdf. Oxford University Press, 2021. Ironically, Muhammad refers to Christians as the Nasara in the Qur'an instead of al-Maseeh, which appropriately identifies believers of the Christian faith in Arabic. Dakdok, *The Generous Qur'an. Surah. 2:62*, 6.

[47] Mark, Joshua J., "Kingdom of Saba. Pg, 6–7." *World History Encyclopedia*. Last modified March 02, 2018. https://www.worldhistory.org/Kingdom_of_Saba/.

[48] Muhammad Muhsin Khan, *The Translation of the Meanings of Sahih Al-Bukhari. Arabic-English. Vol. 1. Ahadith 001 to 875. Hadith 344* (Riyadh, SAE: Darussalam, 2008), 231–2.

[49] Muhammad Muhsin Khan, *The Translation of the Meanings of Sahih Al-Bukhari. Arabic-English. Vol. 5. hadith 4372* (Riyadh, SAE: Darussalam, 2008), 401–2.

tion remains that he stated his conversion to the so-called prophet's "new religion," Islam.

Southern Arab Kingdoms and Bedouin Arabs

Because the Sabean kingdom discussed somewhat covers the southern Arab domains, this section will briefly name those that followed to lead straight into the Bedouins, which ties into the AP deities relevant to Islam's origins. Although the Sabeans identify as the oldest Southern Arabs, other groups such as the Minaeans and Himyaris were influential people. Lesser kingdoms like the Qatabanians and Hadramawt (political and economic influence) still held dominance throughout the south of the Arabian Peninsula.[50]

However, it appears that the immigration of the Bedouin nomadic tribes weakened the Southern Arabian kingdoms' political power and economy significantly over time, leading to the historical Islamization of the AP. Moreover, the observation above seems to be the main driver for the Arabization of the entire AP, which helped immensely create the necessary merge of ethnoreligious identity.[51] Thus, the previous fact shows that the Nabataeans, Sabeans, and every other ethnicity's Arabization today did not only come from the AP's alleged unification under the Abbasid caliphate's necessity of creating a religious theocratic government but also the heavy migratory patterns of the nomadic Arabs.

Interestingly, one should note that as the Nabataeans mentioned above, the Sabeans and other groups south of the AP also had a pantheon of deities. McAuliffe makes an astute observation that out of the many gods in each pantheon known to the peoples of the southern kingdoms, whether Sabian, Qatabanian, Hadramawt, or any other tribe, all worshiped Athtar (McAuliffe, 5).[52] However,

---

[50] Macintosh-Smith, *Arabs*, 50, 52, 70–2. Gibson, The Nabataeans: Builders of Petra., 112–22.

[51] Ibid., *Macintosh-Smith*, 47, 71.

[52] McAuliffe, Jane Dammen. *Encyclopedia of the Qur̄an*. Vol. 6. Leiden: Brill, 2001. Retrieved from: https://scholar.google.ca/scholar?hl=en&as_sdt=0%2C10&q=ancient+pre-islamic+Sabean+Pantheon&btnG=

the Arabian trinity of Allat, Al-Uzza, and Manat were deities known by the eastern and northwestern Arabs until Muhammad's day.[53] Nevertheless, the deities worshiped throughout the Arabic kingdoms, whether in the north, south, or central parts of the AP, were known under different names although representing similar theistic characteristic traits. This would explain some of the gods found in Mecca worshiped by the Quraysh during the existence of Muhammad in its province.

For example, all the Arabic peoples honored Wadd (deity of the moon) in one form or another.[54] Noticeably, Lindstedt names the southern (Himyarite or Yemenite) deity Almaqah as the moon god and Athtar representing the sun, which in this student's view, shows that these deities, among numerous others (as seen in the Nabataean section above), may have different names but maintain the same identities and pagan ritualistic requirements (pp. 12–4, 17).[55] As mentioned earlier in the Nabataean section, Gibson shows how the deities worshiped in the north of the AP were also honored by the southern and Bedouin Arabs, suggesting that the constant interactions between these groups allowed a slow but inevitable religious integration.[56] This author believes Islam is primarily a Judaeo-Christian cult that maintained an Arab paganistic acknowledgment of Allah and his three daughters, Allat, Almanat, and Al-Uzzah. Allah was the name

---

[53] Ibid., 7.

[54] Macintosh-Smith points out that the Minaean deity "Wadd" identifies as the moon god. Macintosh-Smith, *Arabs*, 55.

[55] Lindstedt, Ilkka Juhani. *"Pre-Islamic Arabia and Early Islam." Routledge handbook on early Islam* (2018). Retrieved from: https://helda.helsinki.fi/bitstream/handle/10138/307521/Lindstedt_Early_Muslims_Pre_Islamic_Arabia_and_Pagans_.pdf?sequence=1.

[56] Many Western scholars argue that Allah exists as the legitimate Arabic title recognizing the same biblical God's Lordship. Winfried Corduan, *"Neighboring Faiths: A Christian Introduction to World Religions. Second Edition* (Downers Grove, IL: IVP Academic, 2012), 112–4. However, according to some qur'anic verses, the previous observation appears to be a fallacious claim. Prince points out the theological and linguistic fallacy by demonstrating the Arabic reading of Sur. 4:125. Christian Prince, *El Engaño de Allah (English version, The Deception of Allah)* (Columbia, SC: Christian Prince, 2019), 4–5.

of the principal deity in Mecca who had three daughters. However, many of the English translations of surah 53:19–20 do not read the texts in their original form as written in Arabic due to the theistic insinuation of its content. For example, in the English translation of the respected Islamic scholar Ibn Kathir's comments on the Qur'an, 53:19–22, considered the infamous "satanic verses," state that Allah rebukes the pagan Arabs for rivaling his authority through the goddesses Al-lat, Al-Uzza, and Manat, among other idols. Moreover, the passages also suggest that these deific beings allegedly had the power to manipulate the creation of males for themselves and create the females for Allah despite the latter's preference for the birth of males who could make more Muslim believers.[57]

However, Dakdok, in his English translation of the Qur'an, explicitly states that the original verses (Sur. 53:19–22) highlight Al-lat, Al-Uzza, and Manat, the exalted cranes as intermediaries whose intercession was sought and valued in the eyes of potential Arab believers in Muhammad. Theoretically, the observation above would make Muhammad's qur'anic revelation obsolete because it would make the prophet and his deity's words untrustworthy and erroneous.[58] Still, Prince shows that according to Ibn Hatem's narrative of Muhammad, the prophet bowed before the goddesses with their religious followers in Mecca.[59] After all, if anything said by the Islamic scholar Ibn Kathir stands true, the Arabic reading above highlighting the so-called satanic verses would point to an even more unsavory fact for Muslim adherents regarding the falsity of their alleged prophet Muhammad. Ibn Kathir shows that Satan inspired words into Muhammad's mouth, and he believed them to come from Allah. This means that much of what Muhammad says in the Qur'an or ahadith is untrustworthy.[60]

---

[57] Shaykh Safiur-Rahman Al-Mubarakpuri, *Tafsir Ibn Kathir: Surat Al-Jathiya to the end of Surat Al-Muunafiqun. Abridged. Vol. 9* (Brooklyn, NY: Darussalam, 2003), 318–22.

[58] Dakdok, *The Generous Qur'an. Surah. 53:19–22*, 304.

[59] Prince, *El Engaño de Allah*, 5, 95–7.

[60] Shaykh Safiur-Rahman Al-Mubarakpuri, *Tafsir Ibn Kathir: Surat Al-Isra', Verse 39 to the end of Surat Al-Mu'minun. Abridged. Vol. 6* (Brooklyn, NY: Darussalam,

The Jewish and Sectarian Christian Presence

To this researcher, this section remains one of the most theologically interesting due to the Jewish and Christian monotheistic influences that one can garner from reading the Qur'an, ahadith collections, and tafsirs outlining the beliefs of the prophet Muhammad. Undoubtedly, Arabian monotheism existed, which allegedly frames the theological notions behind the "*hanifs*" mentioned by some Islamic writers. However, one wonders how close it resembles the biblical God's Jewish or Christian theological perspectives (this discussion continues in the sections below). Indeed, the Arab people maintain a legitimate connection to the God of Israel through ancestral lineage.[61] However, the meeting of the previous observations will occur in the following section addressing Muhammad to complete the entire traditional picture leading to the utter delegitimization of the Muslim narrative concerning Qathem's prophetic ministry.[62]

In this thesis, the penned views of John Damascene stand as a valuable asset to those who study Islamic theology in its early stages because he lived among Muslims during his father's employment as a tax collector to the caliph in Damascus, the city of his birth.[63] In his apological works "On Heresies" and *Dialogue between a Saracen and a Christian*, John Damascene viewed the Islamic religion as a strain of Arianism because of its treatment of Jesus Christ as a merely created agent in service of God's purpose for humanity.[64] Additionally, Spencer shows that Damascene had some solid knowledge of chapters found in the Islamic Qur'an today despite possibly not being a completed work during his time.[65] Although this writer deems the

---

61 Maalouf points to Isaac and Ismael at the burial of the Hebrew and Arab patriarch Abraham performing this duty as kin. Maalouf, *Arabs in the Shadow of Israel*, 114, 264.

62 Prince, *El Engaño de Allah*, 9–17, 37.

63 Avery Cardinal Dulles, *A History of Apologetics* (San Francisco, CA: Ignatius Press, 2005), 92.

64 Ibid., 93.

65 Spencer, *Did Muhammad Exist*, 40–3.

observation above trustworthy, it only accounts partially for Islam's theistic views because of two particular components in its belief in their deity Allah.

Pure monotheistic belief comes from the Hebraic culture, which developed amidst the Ancient Near-Eastern peoples' polytheistic environment.[66] The God *Yahweh-Elohim* shows himself to the Hebrew patriarch Abraham through divine revelation, which at times was expressed by a theophany.[67] The Jewish monotheistic view of the biblical God (EL) partially affected "Arab" monotheism much earlier than Christianity because of their Semitic and Abrahamic kinship to the Israeli people.[68] Still, even the previous statement, as the observation before it, only accounts for some of the facts that led to the development of the Islamic religion today.

The observations of Maalouf in this section remain crucial to the issue of Arab monotheism and its relationship to the Jewish monotheistic faith. However, he first connects it to the Ismaeli genealogical line at this point, making sense of the Abrahamic theological heritage passed on to his children Isaac and Ismael.[69] Nevertheless, Maalouf also points out another connection to the Abrahamic faith through the line of Keturah, Abraham's wife after Sarah's death, which remains included in the entirety of God's soteriological plan for the Arabic people.[70] According to Ghillany, the Midianite-Kenite hypothesis suggests the Israelites' religiosity comes from Moses's encounter with Jethro, the Midianite, later called the Kenite, who supposedly taught him about Yahweh when Moses married his daughter and customar-

---

[66] Gleason L. Archer, *A Survey of Old Testament: Introduction. Revised and Expanded* (Chicago, IL: Moody Publishers, 2007), 123.

[67] Lockman, Genesis 12:1–4, 7; 15:1–21; 17:1–22; 18, 26, 31–2, 34–8.

[68] Prince, *El Engaño de Allah*, 4–5. Daniel Block shows the usage of the epithet El among the peoples of the Ancient Near East (ANE). Block, The *Gods of the Nations*, 19, 44–5, 48–9, 66–8.

[69] Maalouf establishes this Abrahamic connection to the title given to God, "El," by the Ismaeli-Edomite Arabs (e.g., Job) and descendants of Joktan found in the book of Genesis. Maalouf, *Arabs in the Shadow of Israel*, 130–2.

[70] Ibid., 20, 186.

ily assimilated her religious beliefs.[71] However, this Midianite-Kenite theory assumed by Paton immediately appears misleading in the face of biblical evidence showing the knowledge of *Yahweh* during the time of the Hebraic patriarchs and Keturah, the matriarch of the Midianites, Jethro's descendant. Hence, Jethro allegedly led Moses to *Yahweh*, the God of Mt. Sinai, despite the Hebraic knowledge of *Yahweh's* name for 432 years before his time, likely recognized among the enslaved Hebrews in Egypt.[72]

Archer dismisses the antiquated JEDP hypothesis created by Wellhausen, employed to advocate the Midianite-Kenite theory based on Wellhausen's fallacious assumptions.[73] Moreover, Archer outlined Wellhausen's omission of "internal biblical evidence" that naturally argues for Moses's authorship "in a large" part of the Pentateuch due to apparent indicators depicted by events, objects, and codified laws foreign to King Josiah's time or later.[74] Still, although Israel was ethnically Semitic like their Arabic cousins (Ismaelis and Keturans), Moses's union with Sephora the Midianite seems to make even more sense of the kinship between those dwelling near the Sinaitic area who recognized their God, *Yahweh*. Nevertheless, Block argues against the Midianite-Kenite hypothesis by suggesting that despite the Midianites' recognition of *Yahweh*, it appears that they may have identified as a henotheistic society.[75] This thesis would make much

---

[71] Paton explains the significance of the Midianite-Kenite hypothesis by referring to the J and E documents so famously formulated by the Graf-Wellhausen theory (JEDP documents). Paton, Lewis Bayles. "The Origin of Yahweh-Worship in Israel: II." *The Biblical World* 28, no. 2 (1906): 113–127. Retrieved from: https://www.journals.uchicago.edu/doi/pdf/10.1086/473788.

[72] Kitchen explains the antiquity of the proper name of God, Yahweh. K. A. Kitchen, *On the Reliability of the Old Testament* (Grand Rapids, MI: Eerdmans Publishing, 2006), 329–33. Moses as the author of the Pentateuch shows the patriarchs' usage of the name of Yahweh in the previous citation.

[73] Archer, *A Survey of Old Testament Introduction*, 80–7, 93–6, 123, 129–31, 133. Klein et al. also highlight specific scholars who worked to disprove the JEDP theory. William W. Klein, Craig L. Blomberg, and Robert L. Hubbard Jr., *Introduction to Biblical Interpretation. 3rd Ed* (Grand Rapids, MI: Zondervan, 2017), 102–3.

[74] Ibid., 226–35.

[75] Block, the Gods of the Nations, 81.

more sense of the identity of a *Hanif* that later evolved throughout the AP, which conceptualizes the pagan Arabs who recognized one head deity above all others. Thus, the previous observation would categorize it more as henotheism than monolatry or monotheism.

After all, in the Ancient Near Eastern world, the deity-land relationship caused many to either conquer another's land or protect theirs in the name of their gods, which may explain the Midianites' oppression of the Israelites during the time of the Judges.[76] Maalouf's striking observation highlights the early corruption of Arabic monotheism must have caused a departure from its Abrahamic theistic heritage much sooner than some may realize. Starcky highlights the progression from Abrahamic monotheism to a paganization of the name El personifying it with created objects substituting the veneration or worship of the true God of the Jews and first Arabs.[77] Additionally, the spiritual darkness that shrouded Israel's monotheistic worship of God perhaps darkened Arab monotheism further.[78] Interestingly, the Jewish people lived throughout the AP before Jesus's days due to the Babylonian exile, after the fall of Jerusalem, and most likely fled the Christian Byzantine kingdom from persecution.[79]

Undoubtedly, the Jewish people returned somewhat to their theistic roots, but the Arabic people who accepted Islam appear to have delved into spiritual disarray until this day. After the Babylonian captivity, most Jews worshiped God alone and abandoned religious syncretism, as observed in the Jewish sects during the Hellenistic period

---

[76] Maalouf, *Arabs in the Shadow of Israel*, 116–7. Archer shows that strict monotheism came explicitly from the Jewish people. Archer, *A Survey of Old Testament*, 123. Block affirms the previous observation. Block, *Israel*, 220–1.

[77] Tony Maalouf, *Arabs in the Shadow of Israel*, 132.

[78] Maalouf affirms this keen observation showing a connection between the Arab spiritual condition attuned to their kin's spiritual and moral status, Israel. Ibid., 179.

[79] Maalouf points to the various Arabian kingdoms ruled by Jewish leaders, which would explain mass conversions to Judaism and massive Jewish communities before the rise of Islam. Ibid., 187–9, 217. Macintosh-Smith affirms Maalouf's notions by highlighting the Himyarite king's adoption of Judaism during the early sixth century. Macintosh-Smith, *Arabs*, 89.

despite their eschatological variances.[80] However, the Arab peoples worshiped multiple gods during the pre-Islamic era of Jahiliya (unbelief and ignorance). Today, the Islamic faith serves a foreign deity holding deific and ritual commonalities with the Judaeo-Christian God but soteriologically incompatible.[81] Thus, the Jewish presence in Arabia makes sense in this junction, considering the kinship leading to centuries-old interactions between the Arab and Judaic peoples, partially explaining how monotheism may have prevailed in certain Arabic religious groups in the Hijaz.[82] In this writer's view, Islam has worked as a spiritually virulent poison to destroy the heritage and blessings of the Arabic peoples who descended from the Abrahamic lineage, unifying them theologically and militarily to eject foreign powers from the AP and aggressively assault their Jewish and Christian religious rivals.

The second part of this section covers the Christian influence on Arab monotheism and its negative views toward orthodox Christianity's monotheistic teachings. Although some scholars believe that Arab Trinitarian Christians who lived abroad in the Arabian Peninsula influenced the Islamic religion's theistic view of God, this scholar suggests that this notion remains an erroneous Westernized academic opinion. The insightful studies of modern German scholars, among others from the United Kingdom and America, have proven

---

[80] See Richard Bauckham's compelling argument outlining the continuity of Jewish monotheism and Christology throughout its Post-Exilic, Palestinian, and Second Temple Judaic periodical phases. Richard Bauckham, *Jesus and the God of Israel: God Crucified and Other Studies on the New Testament's Christology of Divine Identity* (Grand Rapids, MI: Eerdmans Publishing, 2009), ix, 184–5, 193–6, 241–53.

[81] Douglass Groothuis, *Christian Apologetics: A Comprehensive Case for Biblical Faith* (Downers Grove, IL: IVP Academic, 2011), 599–613.

[82] For example, Jewish communities existed throughout the Arabian Peninsula in places like Yathrib, the ancient name of Medina, where the Banu-Qurayza resided, and other Judaic tribes like the Banu-Nadir. Ibid., 29, 187. Alfred Guillaume, *The Life of Muhammad: A Translation of Ishaq's Sirat Rasul Allah* (Karachi, PAK: Oxford University Press, 2016), 450, 461–6. Joukowsky Institute for Archaeology & the Ancient World. Brown University. *Posted at Oct 14/2007 05:56 PM.* Retrieved from: https://brown.edu/Departments/Joukowsky_Institute/courses/islamicarchaeologyglossary2007/4083.html.

quite helpful in confirming this researcher's belief that sectarian Christianity formulated much of the Islamic monotheistic doctrine in combination with its traditional Arab monotheism. As mentioned earlier, Arabic monotheism became corrupted in its early history. Still, it had a period where the Arab consciousness acknowledged the Jewish God, which they held in common as Semitic peoples.[83]

Another interesting fact about the existence of the biblical God in the Arab consciousness lies in the epithet "El," found in names like Abimael used by the ancient Eastern Arabs and their descendants, corroborating one of the Christian usages attributed to their Divine Triunity.[84] The information above creates the foundation for discussing Arab monotheism's relationship with the orthodox Christian monotheistic teaching. Arabs, like their Jewish and Christian predecessors, believed in the biblical Messianic promises, as seen in passages mentioning their inclusion in restorative and redemptive processes by the Judaeo-Christian God.[85] Thus, *Yeshua HaMashiach's* appearance in Israel during the Hellenistic period and later identifying the Roman Empire initiated a highly significant theistic evolution in the Arabian Peninsula, which integrated Christological doctrines that theoretically suited their Arabic monotheistic traditions. However, the previous observation raises the theological difficulty of identifying which Arabic monotheistic period affirms God's orthodox Christian Trinitarian view. After all, our earlier discussions of

---

[83] Maalouf, *Arabs in the Shadow of Israel*, 132–5.

[84] Abimael means "God (EL) is a father." Ibid., 133, 179–81. None of the ninety-nine names given to Allah make him one to either befriend or father anyone. Yet, the Arab awareness of this fact prevailed in their religious consciousness before the emergence of Islam and the so-called prophet Muhammed who unified the AP theologically. Maalouf highlights the biblically derived divine title of "Elmodad," which communicates this previous concept of God.

[85] Maalouf provides an excellent argument for the Arab awareness of the coming Jewish Messiah by using the Matthean birth narrative of Jesus Christ. He suggests the traditional Christian identification of the "Magi" as Persian wise men or astrologers may not appropriately depict the actual identity of these individuals because the gifts of frankincense and myrrh presented to the Messianic king of Israel points to the rich customs of the Arabic peoples. Ibid., 184–6, 196–7, 201–4, 206, 216–8.

Arab theistic traditions in the sections above covered the monotheistic beliefs of patriarchs like Shem (i.e., Noah's son and father of the Semites); Joktan, father of the Southern Arabians; and Job from the land of Uz with his Edomite-Ishmaelite friends.

The citations above mentioning Maalouf's investigative work show how Job's friends judged his attitude toward God.[86] Nevertheless, the early corruption of Arabic monotheism causing the substitution of their God and the creation of pantheons falsely portraying His divine characteristics initiated a set of fictitious trinities imitating the Divine Triunity later understood by the first Jewish Christians through the Holy Spirit's revelation.[87] Thus, after the rise of Christianity, pre-Islamic Arabia presented theological challenges that led to misunderstanding the biblical God's redemptive promises and divine existential being. Although this researcher will discuss the term *hanif* in the section addressing Muhammad, it makes sense to preemptively mention its Christological contribution to the Arabic conscience, causing an utter rejection of Christ's divinity through the absorption of Arianism. These anti-Trinitarian believers mentioned above fled under dire persecutions employed by the primary Church holding Orthodox Trinitarian doctrines throughout the Western and Byzantine Empires for centuries to the AP and finding a theistically corrupted home in Arab monotheism.

Günter Lüling identifies the term *hanif* with the heretical central Arabian Christians adhering to angelic non-Trinitarian Christological views of Jesus, recognizing Him as a limited creation, pointing to His mortality as a mere man.[88] Lüling makes an enormous contribution to the reinterpretation of the initiation behind monotheistic Islamic

---

[86] The words of Job and his friends Eliphaz, Bildad, and Zophar corroborate that the early Arabs worshiped only one God: The God of the Israelites and their Arabic Ancestors by way of Shem, Ismael, Keturah, and Joktan. Lockman Foundation, *Genesis. 10:22–31, 11; 25:1–18; Job 1:1; 2:11; 4:6, 17–8; 8:1, 3; 11:1, 7, 24–5, 52, 836, 840, 842, 847, 850–1.*

[87] For example, the Christological hymn written or cited by the Apostle Paul in the Philippian epistle reveals that Jesus exists as part of the Divine Triunity, making Him a part of the eternal Godhead. Ibid., *Phil. 2:5–11,* 2089–90.

[88] Günter Lüling, *A Challenge to Islam for Reformation: The Rediscovery and Reliable Reconstruction of a Comprehensive Pre-Islamic Christian Hymnal Hidden in the*

teachings by significantly affirming their angelic views of Jesus Christ under the initial Hannifin concepts of God's "angelic high council" of which the Jewish Messianic figure is recognized as the highest-ranking angel.[89] Thus, as the highest angel of the divine order, God communicates His plans to Jesus. Jesus speaks his goals on earth to humanity and executes heaven's redemptive plan, which remains a foreign concept to Orthodox Christian teaching. Therefore, Luling suggests that calling on Jesus, the head of the angelic counsel, appears synonymous with invoking God Himself.

In Orthodox Christian doctrinal teachings, one should notice that angels cannot redeem humanity but can communicate God's will to them. Secondly, suppose the miraculous incarnation, life, death, and resurrection of Christ took place as some Muslims today believe, according to their ancient literature. In that case, Jesus Christ cannot identify as a mere angel.[90] Thirdly, and more importantly, because Jesus can create and breathe life into inanimate objects per qur'anic and hadith writings, it tells us that He cannot identify as a created being but as "The Creator" Himself, confirming Apostle Paul's observations above placing Him in the eternal Godhead. Considering the information above, this author gathers that the presence of heretical Christian non-Trinitarian doctrine and traditional Arabic monotheism gave rise to the Islamic anti-Christian teachings and sentiment today.

Koran Under Earliest Islamic Reinterpretations (Delhi, IN: Motilal Banarsidass Publishers, 2003), 20–1, 70–1, 340.

[89] Ibid.

[90] Jesus, in these verses, is seen giving life to a bird made of clay, which resembles heretical gnostic teachings (3:49). Notice that surah 4:171 clearly validates the Orthodox Trinitarian doctrine and then utterly denies it. Dakdok, *The Generous Qur'an, Surah. 3:42–50; 4:171,* 34–5, 64.

Muhammad

By necessity, this author will briefly cover the biblical criteria that authenticate the standards of a prophetic figure to verify Muhammad's prophethood. The significance of the ethnic and spiritual connection to Muhammad's prophethood remains essential to establishing his religious legitimacy to the peoples of the AP. Moreover, if Muhammad existed as a prophet called to Jews and Christians, his religious tradition would have to corroborate the scriptural criteria set by the biblical prophets and apostles, who received authentically divine revelation from the biblical God, Yahweh-Elohim.[91] However, before delving into the ethnic identity of Muhammad and his theological claims, this writer must briefly discuss the modernly debated issue, which questions the existence of the infamous Arabian prophet of the Qur'an. After all, if Muhammad did not exist, one must wonder why so much supposedly historical data appeared throughout the following centuries after his death and remained recorded in the Islamic sources.

---

[91] In these biblical passages, God inspires Moses to set the prophetic criteria for recognizing a true prophet. Verses 15 and 18 pointedly refer to the Jewish ethnicity of authentic prophets. Nevertheless, if one continues to read the entirety of the passages cited, the so-called prophet Muhammad failed to comply with much of the prophetic criteria. Moreover, the apostle John stated that every spirit that does not confess Jesus has come in the flesh is not from God. Thus, he suggests we should test the spirits. Lockman Foundation, *Deut. 18:9–22; 1 John. 4:1–6*, 309–10, 2224.

Verifying Muhammad's Existence

This researcher undoubtedly believes that the person known as Muhammad in the Islamic sources existed despite the several voices who suggest otherwise. Nevertheless, the facts that some scholars regarded as good evidence for their reasoning of Muhammad's non-existence in the Meccan province or any other region stand credible and convincing. For example, the Hungarian scholar Ignaz Goldziher suggested that the late arrival of the Hadith collections compiled by the alleged Muslim scholars provided ample time to craft fictitious tales of a figure like Muhammad to affirm a political position or goal requiring the support of the people.[92] Additionally, Wansbrough credibly presents the high possibility that the Qur'an, the most sacred written Islamic source of the Muslims, and the Hadith compilations emerged to create a distinctive religion and tradition that could unify the peoples residing in the AP under an Arabized ethnos.[93] Still, despite the well-informed assessments cited above regarding the more than likely fabrications of the Qur'an and Hadith collections, it may not provide enough evidence to dispel the existence of the alleged Arabian prophet Muhammad.

In this writer's view, employing the hermeneutic principle known as the criterion of embarrassment reasonably increases the possibility that Muhammad lived at some point in history.[94] After all, the alleged facts recorded in the Qur'an and Hadith most likely were not so embarrassing during the seventh century, despite appearing categorically shameful to Muslim apologists living in the West today,

---

[92] Goldziher suggests that the hadith may explain the initial procedural developments of the Islamic theological tradition instead of affirming Islam's historicity. Robert Spencer, *Did Muhammad Exist?* 9–10.

[93] Ibid., 11.

[94] The criterion of embarrassment falls under the dissimilarity literary method of inquiry used to describe and understand the reasoning behind actionable details in ancient historiographical biographies that seem contradictory to the behavioral patterns recorded about an individual, group, or specific culture, initiated by an embarrassing factor. Catherine Cory, *A Voyage Through the New Testament. Custom Edition for Saint Leo University. REL. 110* (Upper Saddle River, NJ: Pearson, 2008), 239.

who attempt to defend their so-called prophets' ethical conduct. For instance, Cory presents Jesus's baptism by John the Baptist as a prime example. Many in the ancient world would have considered the act of Jesus being baptized by John as an embarrassment because it suggests inferiority and sinfulness at first glance if one remains at a superficial level of inquiry.[95] Thus, like the example provided by the New Testament illustration, it appears an appropriate comparison to the many acts of Muhammad that contradict the Muslim narratives contrived in the West about their prophet's "goodness," countering the Judaeo-Christian ethics by which Western nations established their norms.

However, this thesis suggests that the Arabian prophet may not have come from the Meccan province as many modern Muslims assume out of sheer traditional values taught by ancestral Islamic believers. Secondly, for Muhammad's legend to become important enough for the Muslim community to deem it necessary to write the sunnah, hadith, and Qur'an (in this writer's opinion, an additional hadith collection) frames this action as a product of historical momentum. Thus, no one in their right mind would have invented Muhammad's immoral and unethical personality to unify the Arabian Peninsula two hundred years later with what many in the Western and Eastern Empires would consider as thoroughly morally abhorrent behavior. However, because Muhammad's conduct historically aligned with the religious and raiding practices of the Arabs described in their poetry and inscriptions found on rocks and walls discovered by archaeologists, it points to the probability that he did exist, although not in the Mecca as described by the Islamic narrative sources.

In this writer's opinion, Muhammad's immoral behaviors align with any typical seventh-century warlord from the AP or any other place in the ancient world. However, the main problem is that no documentation about Muhammad existed until two hundred years after

---

[95] Ibid.

his alleged death.[96] However, as stated earlier, historic momentum plays an enormous role in establishing Muhammad's existence, especially in an orally oriented culture like the Arabic peoples, as shown in the sections above to explain the variances between the many written sources. In Köstenberger et al.'s refutation of Bart Ehrman's work against the New Testament's Gospel narratives' validity as an authentically God-inspired work, they advocate for the genuine worth of the biblical record by highlighting that the first-century culture was orally oriented.[97] Although unrelated to Köstenberger et al.'s observation above, one should note that Islamic culture "allegedly" kept the oral tradition alive. However, no living witness could confirm any supposed tradition's integrity, making Hadith compilations inapplicable.

During the seventh and eighth centuries, when qur'anic literature referred to the Jews and Christians as "people of the book," it indicated that Arab Muslims did not have a centralized religious book outside of Arabic poetic literature or theistic inscriptions.[98] Still, most chain narrations maintain parallel sayings and acts enacted by this mythical Arabian figure, Muhammad.[99] Nevertheless, according to

---

[96] Peter Webb points out that Islamic sources appeared in Iraq three hundred years after the fall of the Byzantines and Sasanians. Webb, *Imagining the Arabs*, 78. Spencer highlights those writings about Muhammad that appear two hundred to three hundred years later than when he allegedly lived. Moreover, the Islamic law scholar Joseph Schacht suggests that the earliest records scantly appear in the first decades of the eighth century AD. Robert Spencer, *Did Muhammad Exist?* xvi, 7, 11.

[97] Köstenberger, *Truth in a Culture of Doubt*, 58.

[98] Muhammad Taqi-ud-Din Al-Hilali and Muhammad Muhsin Khan, *Interpretations of The Meanings of The Noble Qur'an in The English Language: A Summarized Version of At-Tabari, Al-Qurtubi, and Ibn Kathir with Comments from Sahih Al-Bukhari. Vol. 1. Surah. 3:98–9* (Riyadh, SAU: Darussalam, 1996), 93. Luxenberg affirms that no established Arabic literature existed outside of sporadic scripts. Christoph Luxenberg, *The Syro-Aramaic Reading of the Koran*, 30.

[99] For example, despite the variances in the so-called Islamic scholarly commentaries about the specific sunnah of Muhammad, they mostly agree on his actions and sayings. Touching and even worshiping the venerated black stone by Muhammad is one of the actions recorded by the revered Islamic scholars. Muhammad, Khan. *The Translation of The Meanings of Sahih Al-Bukhari, Vol.*

the information cited above, one should consider that multiple attestations in the case of Islamic sources could remain irrelevant because of its two- to three-hundred-year removal from any living eyewitness that allegedly lived during Muhammad's time. Köstenberger et al. rightly state that the criterion of multiple attestations validates historical claims by finding similar events in various external literary sources of the same period affirming them. However, in their application of this hermeneutic technique to the Gospel narratives, they observe that having "eyewitnesses" initially recording the actual event would bolster the validation of its authenticity, which, in the case of Islamic sources, does not exist.[100] The topic presented in the statement above will continue in the section below under the discussion of the Islamic Qur'an.

As stated earlier, this writer believes that although the figure of Muhammad remains an actual person, he did not exist as the infamous Arabian prophet of Meccan origin. Indeed, the Qur'an itself (as cited in earlier sections) allegedly quotes Allah telling Muhammad that he passes by the ruins of Sodom and Gomorrah every morning and reflects on its destruction at night.[101] Hence, for this researcher, this qur'anic quotation alone causes one to ponder the two specific details salient to discovering the ethnic identity of Muhammad and the origins of his religious beliefs and practices. According to the Sira of Muhammad, written by Ibn Ishaq, the lineage of Muhammad comes directly from Ismael, son of the Hebrew patriarch Abraham.[102] However, even if one grants Muhammad an Ismaili line of descendance for argument's sake, genealogical difficulties still arise because

---

2, Book 25, Hadith. 1597, 1605, 1607, 1609–12. (Riyadh, SAE: Darussalam, 2008), 385, 389–91. Imam Abul Hussain Muslim bin Al-Hajjaj et al., *English Translation of Sahih Muslim. Vol. 6. From Hadith no. 5646 to 6722. [6359] 132-(2473)* (Brooklyn, NY: Darussalam, 2007), 334.

[100] Köstenberger, et al., *Truth in a Culture of Doubt*, 62–3.

[101] See footnote 25 and 26.

[102] Allegedly, Muhammad ordered Malik al-Ansari (al-Sulami) to show compassion for the Egyptians during their conquest because of their kinship to Hagar the Egyptian through Ismail, their progenitor. Alfred Guillaume, *The Life of Muhammad: A Translation of Ishaq's Sirat Rasul Allah* (Karachi, PAK: Oxford University Press, 2016), 3–4.

no one can confidently identify his biological father. However, this conversation will continue in the paragraphs below, covering the significance of Muhammad's name.

Firstly, *Muhammad* is a title and not a name. The Arabian prophet's name derives from a divine depiction of God, making this a theistic association. Prince highlights the meaning of the name *Muhammad*, which can only apply to God or, in this case, the Islamic deity Allah.[103] This researcher believes that Surah 4:80 and 61:6 show Prince's assertion above of the title used by the so-called Arabian prophet because the latter ayat shows the name "Ahmed," meaning "the praised one," a variation of the name *Muhammad*. At the same time, the former enforces and qualifies obedience to the Arabian prophet as equal to obeying the deity Allah.

Spencer confirms the above by referring to the work of Alfred Guillaume, suggesting that the designation of the term *Ahmed* initially applied to Jesus Christ Himself instead of Qathem, the so-called Arabian prophet.[104] Thus, according to the Muslims themselves, Muhammad's name would theoretically categorize as a blasphemous designation, making a human being equal to Allah.[105] Therefore, one wonders if the millions of Muslim men carrying the Christ title Muhammad as a name understand the spiritual ramifications of using it while identifying and glorifying themselves as the divine being they worship (see footnotes 103–104).

Indeed, the three previous observations become a theological contradiction unless Muslims believe that Muhammad identifies as "the" divine (not "divinely appointed") messianic figure. Yet whenever a Muslim (more specifically Sunnis and others resembling their Islamic practice) says the *shahada* (e.g., there is no God but Allah,

---

[103] Moreover, Prince makes a "clad iron" case showing the reasons behind using the title "Muhammad" by Qathem, whose genealogical origins remain somewhat nebulous. Christian Prince, *El Engaño de Allah*, 38–9.

[104] Robert Spencer, *Did Muhammad Exist?* 49.

[105] The Islamic scholar Al-Jalalayn speaks about the severity of associating men or angels with Allah. Aisha Bewley, Abdalhaqq Bewley, and Muhammad Isa Waley, *Tafsir Al-Jalalayn. Al-Maida (Surah. 3:64, 80; 5:17, 69, 72–3)* (London, UK: Dar Al Taqwa Ltd., 2014), 134, 138, 243, 262.

and Muhammad is his prophet, pronounced in the Arabic, *la ilaha illa Allahu wa anna Muhammad Rasul Allah*), they must associate Muhammad with Allah for the opportunity of salvation to become enacted.[106] Ironically, that would designate him as part of some deific unity, like those of the pagan Arabs or the eternal Godhead recognized by Christians as the Holy Trinitarian God. Therefore, this writer agrees with Prince's assessment that Qathem changed his name to Muhammad to assert his prophetic authority that is unchallenged by the pagan Arabs and others like the monotheistic Jewish people and sectarian Christians residing in Mecca and Medina (see footnote 103).

However, to this writer, Mecca as the designated location of Muhammad's prophetic ministry remains questionable despite the multiple attestations provided by the Islamic sources, written two to three hundred years after the fact. Still, as discussed earlier, historic momentum makes Muhammad (Qathem) an actual person confirmed by many sources. Some believe he lived in the seventh century and perhaps at an earlier date while others think him not ethnically Arab or of Ismaeli descent.[107] Thus, for the rest of this section, we will discover the ethnic and genealogical origins of Qathem and the likely practices passed onto Islamic theologically based rituals. As stated in earlier sections of this thesis, the tribe of Muhammad, the Quraysh, had the name of "shark" or some similar sea creature, which seems an odd moniker for a "desert-dwelling" tribe!

Indeed, this observation tells us that perhaps the beginnings of the so-called prophet Muhammad began elsewhere outside of the Meccan province because it neither had a shore, mountains, nor "sharks"; it was a desert. Hence, some of the depictions in the had-

---

[106] Muhammad Muhsin Khan, *The Translation of the Meanings of Sahih Al-Bukhari. Arabic-English. Vol. Ahadith 001 to 875. Hadith 25* (Riyadh, SAE: Darussalam, 2008), 66.

[107] Spencer presents striking evidence of coinage and religious symbols and structures, which neither shows any Islamic doctrinal beliefs nor mentions Muhammad as Allah's prophet. Robert Spencer, *Did Muhammad Exist?* 6–7, 45–58. Indeed, the ethnic-Arab identity of the so-called prophet Muhammad appears contrived much later.

ith and Qur'an tell us that perhaps Muhammad may have worked his way into the Meccan province through trade and established a life there. However, theistically speaking, the Arab monotheism he proclaimed had probably preexisted, as we can see by the coinage in Spencer's observations and the work presented by Luling above (see citation 107).

Continuing the conversation that began in the previous paragraphs, the contrived genealogy of Muhammad provided by Alfred Guillaume's translation of Ibn Isham's work creates too many difficulties for his alleged lineage and prophetic legitimacy because it casts an enormous shadow on the validity of modern Islamic claims. First, the entire Muhammadan Islamic religion hinges on the Arabian prophet's Ismaeli lineage instead of Keturah's, as a son of Abraham. The Sira of Muhammad attempts to validate his connection to Ismael and overemphasizes it so much that Ibn Ishaq traces his genealogy beyond Abraham to Adam (see footnote 102).

Oddly, this above observation attempts to imitate the Matthean illustration of Jesus Christ's genealogy as evidence of His Messiahship. Brown eloquently highlights how the Matthean genealogy of *Yeshua* represented the genesis concept of "origins," setting the preface for connecting the ancestral beginnings of the Judaic Messianic figure to a "new creation" representing Him as more excellent than the old regarding His redemptive mission in the world. According to Brown, the observation above is done by an intentional play of the Greek verb *egenneson* (begot), pointing to the miraculous birth of Christ by also connecting this concept to its opening phrase in his Gospel, *geneseos* (Matthew 1:1).[108] On the other hand, the Muhammad genealogical narrative fails miserably to connect any theological connotations to any legitimate prophetic line (e.g., King David stands as the legitimate ancestor of Jesus, making him a descendant of the house of

---

[108] Raymond E. Brown, *An Introduction to the New Testament* (New Haven, CT: Yale Aybrl, 2010), 174–5. However, the title of Muhammad applied to Qathem, the mysteriously adopted son should solely apply to the expected Messianic figure forming part of the eternal Godhead. Prince states that Qathem himself usurped the title of Muhammad around his thirtieth birthday (as discussed above).

David and the tribe of Judah who the Bible says that his descendant will "rule with a scepter that shall not leave his hand").[109]

Ibn Ishaq fails miserably for two reasons. One, although the descendants of Ismael are grouped as Arabs today, it does not necessarily seem to be the case because, as we discussed earlier, the Nabateans, which appear to descend from the Ismaeli line, did not consider themselves Arab and moved into Edomite Petrean land in the north. Furthermore, to "fix" the prevalent genealogical issue that exists with naming Abdullah as Muhammad's father and Amina as his mother (although Amina remains the likely maternal candidate), the prophet's paternal line does not fit the Muslim narrative, and neither does the "four-year" pregnancy.[110]

Prince makes an excellent and informative contribution with his detailed analysis of Muhammad's identity by highlighting that no one can know whether his alleged grandfather or designated father (according to the information provided by the Islamic sources) was the actual paternal figure. Nevertheless, despite both men sleeping with Muhammad's mother, Amina, Khadija's cousin, Waraqa Ibn Nawfal, the sectarian Christian priest, tried keeping Amina for himself.[111] Hence, in this researcher's opinion, it remains highly probable that Waraqa Ibn Nawfal was identified as Qathem's birth father, which would explain Muhammad's suicidal tendencies when Waraqa passed away because he no longer received qur'anic inspiration.[112] Secondly, according to the biblical criteria set as a standard for recognizing prophets sent by *YHWH-ELOHIM*, it could not validate Muhammad's prophethood because he did not descend from the Hebraic line of prophets. Moreover, most of Muhammad's proph-

---

[109] Lockman Foundation, *Genesis. 49:10; Num. 24:17; Psalm. 60:7,* 97, 261, 956.

[110] Dakdok points out that the alleged father designated to Qathem (Muhammad) died four years before birth. Usama K. Dakdok, *Exposing the Truth About the Qur'an: The Revelation of Error. The Stories of the Prophets. Vol. 2 of 2* (Venice, FL: Usama Dakdok Publishing, 2013), 278–9. Hence, in this researcher's opinion, it remains highly probable that Waraqa Ibn Nawfal was identified as Qathem's birth father, which would explain Muhammad's suicidal tendencies when Waraqa passed away and no longer received qur'anic inspiration.

[111] Christian Prince, *El Engaño de Allah,* 9–18.

[112] Guillaume, *The Life of Muhammad,* 68–9.

ecies and religious beliefs that make Islam stand on par with the Jewish and Christian scripturally prophetic and theistic doctrines were proven false.[113] Remember, if we accept the narrative of Ibn Ishaq and other Islamic scholars like Al-Qurtubi or Al-Tabari as most Muslims, then the Ismaeli lineage does not provide enough theological support to establish prophethood to the Arabic people nor universally to all of humanity.[114]

Considering the norms above and the fact that those residing in the Meccan and Medinan provinces appear to descend from the line of Keturah, Abraham's second wife (again, following Mecca's alleged primary role), who migrated to Central Arabia, implicates Muhammad as a rogue prophet against God's order (see footnote 11–12, 68–69). Thus, the following section will further elaborate on the origins of Muhammad's strange reception of the alleged qur'anic scriptures and whether its patterns resembled previous prophets of the Jewish nation. Nevertheless, as stated earlier, Islam does not identify all Arab peoples. Still, it serves as a deific curse affecting their worldwide affairs and relations with others who do not ascribe to this Arabized Judaeo-Christian cult. However, like many modern-day Jewish and Christian believers lacking knowledge of their theology, many Muslims adhering to the Islamic teachings behave much better than the portrayal of their prophet Muhammad pre-

---

[113] Out of several examples one can use, in surah 30:2–4, Muhammad predicts the Roman defeat and victory over the Persians. However, the problem lies in that these things had already occurred. Moreover, according to Dakdok, the writing of this previous observation occurred after Uthman burned the alleged original Qur'an, which places an even further strain on its integrity. Dakdok, *Exposing the Truth About the Qur'an. Vol. 2 of 2*, 323–4.

[114] One of the most respected Islamic scholars among the Sunnis, Ibn Kathir, wrote and explicitly taught in his Tafsir that Muhammad stands as the universal prophet placing him above all others. Shaykh Safiur-Rahman Al-Mubarakpuri, *Tafsir Ibn Kathir: Surat Al-A'raf, to the end of Surat Yunus. Abridged. Vol. 4* (Brooklyn, NY: Darussalam, 2003), 182–3. However, several verses from *The Generous Qur'an* contradict and undermine Muhammad's universality because they state that Allah makes no distinctions among them. Islamic theology claims, that prophets are sent "only" to their respective lands because they speak the tongue of the province. Usama Dakdok, *The Generous Qur'an. Surah 2:136; 3:83–4; 7:158; 14:4, 14, 37–8, 102*, 149.

sented in their sacred writings (i.e., the Qur'an, ahadith, and taf-sirs). Thus, this shows an Abrahamic-based morality in the Middle Eastern conscience going back to the ancient Semitic recognition that all of humanity remains accountable to one God, despite the qur'anic mandate to imitate Muhammad's conduct.[115]

Muhammad's Prophethood

The origins of Islam remain the focal point of this thesis, and this section will remain brief. However, Muhammad's first marriage has everything to do with his prophethood. It will affirm all the information in the paragraphs above regarding this researcher's earlier statements suggesting that Islam emerged as an Arabized Judaeo-Christian cult in the Arabian Peninsula. This writer readily admits that despite the hermeneutic, historical, and archaeological contributions of several brilliant authors mentioned above, it remains highly probable that the actions described in Islamic sources about Muhammad make him a historical reality. Moreover, this researcher presented religious, genealogical, and geographical facts about the pre-Islamic cultures that may lead one to conclude that the Arabian prophet may not have started his ministry in Mecca. However, traditional Islamic sources and most mainstream academics, whether Western, Eastern, or Middle Eastern, have accepted the Muslim narrative as historical fact, affirming Muhammad's Meccan beginnings.[116]

Nevertheless, our concern here does not dwell on the traditional dates of Muhammad's birth or marriages due to all the dubious information presented above or his career before acquiring fame as the

---

[115] Usama Dakdok, *The Generous Qur'an. Surah. 33:21*, 243.

[116] Despite the mainstream academic acceptance of the historical narratives presented in the Islamic sources, Peter Webb's investigative work on the absence of "Arabness" in pre-Islamic Arabia appears to affirm this researcher's opinion that Muhammad's entire story probably took place in another time and place outside of the Meccan area. Webb states that the caliphates reconstructed pre-Islamic reports describing actual people and events of the past and applied them to other personalities during the Islamic era to create a societally centralized Arab identity in the conquered lands like Iraq, Syria, and the Hijaz. Webb, *Imagining the Arabs*, 88, 252, 330.

Arabian prophet. However, the reality of Islam's rise to power in the world due to an alleged revelation from the Islamic deity Allah to the prophetic figure Muhammad should raise the theological curiosity of all seeking the truth about this individual's experiential claims, which occurs during his marriage to his first wife, Khadija.[117] This writer observes that Muhammad's union with Khadija "resembles" the Christian marriages between one man and woman. Although previously married, Khadija may have had the sectarian Christian influence of her cousin Waraqa Ibn Nawfal, the rogue priest. In contrast, those mandated and depicted in the Qur'an by the Arabian prophet never use the word for marriage but the vulgar word representing the sexual act instead.[118] Indeed, this shows a noticeable behavioral change in the character of Muhammad in his later years, at least, according to ahadith materials and the sira. Thus, the question remains whether the death of Khadija caused this change or his newfound divine revelation.

Unquestionably, one immediately observes the strange, if not malefic, way Muhammad receives the divine revelation in an encounter he supposedly has with an angelic being. However, when the Jewish prophets of the Old Testament received God's message, they sometimes acted out the prophetic word, illustrating to their audiences how He would enact His judgment in the future on the people to whom it directed itself.[119] Moreover, although they received the Word of God with fear (respect) and trembling (submission) as they stood in awe of God's supernatural power revealing the future events or addressing current societal affairs, this did not include demonic manifestations or confusion causing mixed messages. We can observe

---

[117] The Caner brothers affirm Muhammad's twenty-five-year marriage to Khadija. After Khadija's death, Muhammad married twelve other women. Ergun Mehmet Caner and Emir Fethi Caner, *Unveiling Islam: An Insider's look at Muslim Life and Beliefs. Updated and Expanded Edition* (Grand Rapids, MI: Kregel Publications, 2009), 39–40, 55–6.

[118] Christian Prince, *Sex & Allah. Vol. I* (Columbia, SC: Christian Prince, 2018), 6–7, 11. Usama Dakdok, *The Generous Qur'an. Surah. 4:3, 24–5, 47, 50.*

[119] Corrine L. Carvalho, *Encountering Ancient Voices: A Guide to Reading the Old Testament. 2ⁿᵈ Ed* (Winona, MN: Anselm Academic, 2010), 245–7.

various biblical accounts demonstrating in detail the effects of human exposure to the supernatural power of the divine.

First, as Isaiah experienced his heavenly vision and felt God's overwhelming metaphysical presence, he immediately realized his sinful condition and mortality contrasting God's eternally royal authority and power. Moreover, the prophet Ezekiel fell to his face in awe of observing heavenly realities beyond his physical capacities. Lastly, when Daniel encountered the supernatural presence of the archangel Gabriel during his reception of God's prophetic message, the impact caused Daniel to fear and even become physically sick for days. Notice that the passages cited in Daniel show no confusion after the angel explains the visions. However, Daniel's mortal body experienced weakness during his exposure to Gabriel and the futuristic message.[120]

However, Muhammad was physically abused and mentally tormented. He needed Khadija's sensual pagan ritual to discern whether the messenger from beyond came from their Allah or perhaps shaitan and thought himself possessed. Moreover, after Khadija and Muhammad's nude sexual pagan performance, Waraqa Ibn Nawfal, the rogue Christian sectarian priest, erroneously tells them that Muhammad's "angelic" encounter was with the same angel who presented himself to the prophet Moses.[121] Indeed, Muhammad's disturbingly suicidal behavior and disorder were demonstrated when he continually needed affirmation of his prophethood and later after his trustworthy source of the Qur'an died, Waraqa Ibn Nawfal.[122]

If the Muslim sources speak the truth, Muhammad's prophethood begins on a sour note in the cave at Hira and during the initial days of his ministry in Mecca. Although the popular Muslim nar-

---

120 The Lockman Foundation, *Isaiah. 6:5–7; Ezek. 1:28; 2:1; Dan. 8:15–9, 27*, 1147, 1348, 1440–1.

121 Alfred Guillaume, *The Life of Muhammad*, 105–6. Muhammad Muhsin Khan, *The Translation of The Meanings of Sahih Al-Bukhari, Vol. 4. Ahadith 2738 to 3648 [Book 60. 3392]* (Riyadh, SAE. Darussalam, 2008), 372–3.

122 Usama K. Dakdok, *Exposing the Truth About the Qur'an: The Revelation of Error. The Stories of the Prophets. Vol. 2 of 2*, 322. Alfred Guillaume, The Life of Muhammad, 106.

rative says that the Quraysh began mistreating Muhammad and his believers, it was his followers who drew first blood when they murdered a polytheist. Muhammad lived peacefully for approximately twelve years among his tribesman, the pagan Quraysh, and they began believing in Islam until he insulted their gods.[123] Moreover, his life ends with a terrible melody of pain according to his depiction of how a false prophet dies, despite all of his impressive accomplishments in unifying the Arab peoples by convincing the appropriate "disciples.[124]" Muhammad's Islamic warriors would carry forth his religious beliefs with such massive bloodlust that they were able to conquer immense swaths of Arab, Jewish, Christian, and Persian lands in a concise amount of time.[125] As stated earlier, Muhammad's identity as a Meccan Arab remains questionable, although, in this writer's view, this person existed, and his actions undoubtedly happened. After all, historical momentum remains an undeniable factor.

The point of bringing up the previous observations in this section of Muhammad's prophethood is to briefly highlight the origins of Islam's spiritual founding, which to this author, appears demonic, veering off from the initial Arabic monotheistic conviction early in the history of the Arab patriarchs like Ismael, Job, or Joktan from Keturah's genealogical line. As stated earlier in this thesis, Arabic monotheism became corrupted early on. Still, in this author's opinion, Muhammad's creation of today's Islamic religion founded itself on a poisonous deception hitching itself to Abraham's authentic faith in *Yahweh-Elohim*.

---

[123] Ibid., Khan, 118–9. Usama K. Dakdok, *Exposing the Truth About the Qur'an: The Revelation of Error. The Stories of the Prophets. Vol. 2 of 2*, 294–5.

[124] Ibid., 336–8. Usama Dakdok, *The Generous Qur'an. Surah. 69:44–6*, 332. Oddly, ("Allah") Muhammad states in the Qur'an that his deity would sever the aorta of any claiming themselves a prophet falsely, and yet, his child-bride Aisha revealed that Muhammad painfully expressed that he felt his aorta was being cut. Muhammad Muhsin Khan, *The Translation of the Meanings of Sahih Al-Bukhari. Arabic-English. Vol. 5. Ahadith 3649 to 4473. hadith 4428* (Riyadh, SAE. Darussalam, 2008), 437.

[125] Robert Spencer, *The History of Jihad: From Muhammad to Isis* (New York, NY: Bombardier Books, 2018), 16–7, 22–4, 28–31, 52–66.

Thus, to this researcher, the revelation of the Qur'an appears at least a written plan sporadically driven by a demoniacally manipulated man who God did not approve of, and his mission seemed like that of Nimrod's, "the first mighty hunter before the Lord."[126] This author compares Muhammad to Nimrod because both appear as "mighty hunters" of humanity's souls before the Lord God. They sought to confuse and redirect the souls of human beings against the true God *Yahweh-Elohim* by constructing an idolatrous narrative causing deific deception. This researcher makes the speculative assertion because although we do not know much about Nimrod, he appears to be the founder of the oldest cities of Mesopotamia (e.g., Babel), which seem to be the birthplace of the Ancient Near Eastern religions that rebelled against the monotheistic revelation of God and perverted the worship of El.[127] Thus, although Jewish and Christian influence shaped the Islamic notion of tawhid regarding Muhammad's Allah, the Muslim deity resembles the infamous pre-Islamic moon god Hubal, worshiped during pre-Islamic times who opposed the *Yahweh-Elohim* of Israel as Baal.[128] Indeed, the

---

[126] Aisha, the child bride of Muhammad, narrated that some of his companions observed and heard how Muhammad received the alleged divine revelation, which eerily paralleled demonic possession. Hafiz Abu Tahir Zubair "Ali Za'i, Nasiruddin Al-Khattab, and Abu Khaliyl, *English Translation of Sahih Muslim Compiled by: Imam Abul Hussain Muslim Ibn al-Hajjaj. Vol. 6. [6058] 86 – (2333), [6059] 87, [6060] 88 – (2334)* (Brooklyn, NY: Darussalam, 2007), 181–2.

[127] This author believes that Nimrod as the founder of "Babel," created it as the epicenter of theistic confusion by its focus on human independence from Elohim and the bridge to every world religion, which incidentally, the name of Baal appears at times referring to rulers as divine or the actual divinity. Jay P. Green Sr., *The Interlinear Bible: Hebrew, Greek, and English with Strong's Concordance Numbers Above Each Word. Genesis. 10:8–11; 11:1–9* (Peabody, MA: Hendrickson Publishers, 2008), 8–9. Block, *The Gods of the Nations*, 50, 52, 61–4. Sam Shamoun, *Answering Islam: Revisiting the Identity of the Pre-Islamic Allah at Mecca Pt. 1. Pg. 10–4.* Retrieved from: https://answering-islam. org/authors/shamoun/preislamic_allah1.html.

[128] Shamoun highlights that the name Hubal, the highest deity worshiped by ancient Meccan Arabs, was a corruption of the moniker ha-Baal, previously used by the Nabataeans, which remained the god of the Kaaba by morphing into the current name of Allah. Ibid., Shamoun.

Islamic deity Allah and his so-called prophet Muhammad continue to fight the Judaeo-Christian God until this day by targeting them through "deific mandates" until they confess them as God and prophet, resembling the old rivalry between Baal and Yahweh worship throughout Israel's history.[129]

As seen in some of the paragraphs and citations above, Muhammad's prophethood was spiritually compromised in its inception according to the Judaic and Christian standards. Muhammad received revelation from a demonic being, performed and incorporated pagan Arab rituals, bowed before the pagan Arab gods, and initially favored the Jewish, Christian, and Sabian believers to gain the support of all these religious groups.[130] The previous observation shows that Muhammad lies to attain favor, which remains an acceptable action in the Islamic doctrine of taqiyya today.[131] As they rejected Muhammad's appeal to the Abrahamic faith for prophetic authentication, each of the groups mentioned above was either expelled from their homes and lands or relegated to an utter submission to his religious leanings through rape, pillaging, and ultimate humiliation, as shown earlier.

For these reasons, the figure of Muhammad related to the historical acts described above demonstrates historical momentum despite the brilliant work of many modern Christian scholars. Moreover, like most cult leaders, Qathem pressed on to attain riches, sex, and power to gain an artificially constructed favorability among the people by distorting God's truth through reframing alienation, theological compromise, and utter conquest of all who opposed his fictitious prophetic title bestowed on himself. For example, we observe spiritually compromising and sexually polygamous behaviors in cult leaders like Joseph Smith, the founder of the Mormons. Although Muhammad's culture was polygamous, he did not practice the tradition until Khadija's death, and yet, like Smith, he began

---

[129] The Lockman Foundation, 1ˢᵗ Kings.

[130] Dakdok, *The Generous Qur'an. 2:62, 158; 3:113; 5:69, 89; 22:17; 53:19–23, 6–7, 15–6, 40, 72, 194, 304.*

[131] Aisha Bewley, Abdalhaqq Bewley, and Muhammad Isa Waley, *Tafsir Al-Jalalayn. Al-Maida, Surah. 5:89,* 267.

practicing polygamy after the "cave experience" where the imaginary angel Moroni presented him with golden tablets, also distorted biblical scriptures and created fictitious revelations to justify his religious authenticity as a modern-day prophet.[132] Qathem, the originator of Islam, had nothing uniquely original to offer the world because despite the conceptual tawhid ("one of" forming a unity) he confessed to the Arabs highlighting Abrahamic monotheism, he still believed in other deities and affirmed them as other creators competing with the god Allah.[133]

Concerning the usurpation of Muhammad's divine title, perhaps Qathem intentionally wanted to impersonate the deific and incarnate Messianic figure Jesus Christ to authenticate his prophetic ministry. Still, the noticeable issue in the Muhammadan religion remains its "unmiraculous" origins despite the claim of identifying the Qur'an as a miracle.[134] Nevertheless, this discussion will continue in the section below. However, Islam's originator seemed to initiate its theology through the alleged Hannifin Arabic monotheistic cult, which remains an oddity due to the nature of the word because it implicated a paganized origin that recognized one God while simultaneously acknowledging other deities as metaphysical entities. Although this researcher agrees with Warraq concerning the initial meaning of the word *hanif* and its later intended usage of disassociating itself from idolatry, it poses extreme difficulties because the word goes back to the days when Abraham was an idolater.[135] Still, this writer corroborates Warraq's earlier notion that the pre-Islamic monotheistic concept was neither Jewish nor Christian. Thus, in

---

[132] Ron Rhodes and Marian Bodine, *Reasoning from the Scriptures with the Mormons* (Eugene, OR: Harvest House Publishers, 1995), 21–7.

[133] One cannot help noticing a peculiar trait between the two cults of Islam and early Mormonism. Although outwardly, at a superficial level, Islam and Mormonism confess to only one God, they believe in many others. Ibid., 243–7. Bewley, Bewley, and Waley, *Tafsir Al-Jalalayn. Al-Mu'minun, the Believers. Surah. 23:14*, 730–1.

[134] Hafiz Abu Tahir Zubair Za'I, "Ali, Al-Khattab, Nasiruddin, and Khaliyl, Abu, *English Translation of Sahih Muslim Compiled by: Imam Abul Hussain Muslim Ibn al-Hajjaj. Vol. 1. [385] 239-(152)* (Brooklyn, NY: Darussalam, 2007), 243.

[135] Warraq, *What the Koran Really Says*, 134–6, 189.

this student's view, the person who usurped the title "Muhammad" took advantage of the familiar term in the theistically Arabic theistic microcosm and placed Judaeo-Christian ideological connotations to create a theological distinction from its Jewish Christian predecessors.

By reinterpreting the qur'anic usage of the Arabic phrase *hanif* through a Syro-Aramaic reading of the term (*hanpa*), Luxenberg somewhat affirms this writer's notion of the word's association with Abraham as a heathen before his commitment to obey *Yahweh-Elohim*. Luxenberg's definition of the word *hanif* convinces this researcher's theoretic conviction that the Arabian prophet Muhammad applied this term to himself and those who followed him to distinguish his new religion from the existent Jewish and Christian monotheistic faiths. However, Luxenberg observes that like Abraham recognizing God while he still held to heathenism, suggesting the existence of other deities in the Ancient Near East, Muhammad perhaps identified Allah as the only legitimate deity. In contrast, all others remained submitted to Allah's will. Thus, by this researcher's previous observation, one could perceive how Arabic monotheism in its pre-Islamic and Islamic form would definitively differ from Jewish or Christian monotheistic beliefs while maintaining similarities with the sects of these religions.[136] Thus, according to the biblical criteria cited in the sections above for the validation of a prophet, Muhammad could have never qualified, which remains the reason for his rejection by most Jews and Christians of his time.

---

[136] Christoph Luxenberg, *The Syro-Aramaic Reading of the Koran*, 55–6.

The Quran

For all Muslims worldwide, the Qur'an remains the most sacred book of the Islamic faith. Many refer to the Qur'an as the *Umm al Kitab*, meaning, "the mother of the book," perfectly preserved because of its alleged heavenly origin.[137] Muhammad's mandates found in the Qur'an were supposedly inspired by the deity Allah and, therefore, revered by Muslims as applicable to all quotidian life activities and the jurisprudential framework setting the premise for societal laws in Islamic countries. Valkenberg places the Qur'an as the primary source and center of all legal interpretations in Islamic countries.[138] Thus, the Qur'an is the most significant component of Islamic civilization for the morality behind all judicial precedent, societal conduct, and religious practice applied and imposed on all its citizens, whether Muslim believers or non-Muslims.

---

[137] The qur'anic ayat making this reference and establishing the Qur'an as divine lie in surah 3:7 and 85:21–2. Bewley, Bewley, and Waley, *Tafsir Al-Jalalayn.*, 116, 1314. 111. Safiur-Rahman Al-Mubarakpuri. *Tafsir Ibn Kathir: Surat Al-Jathiya to the end of Surat Al-Muunafiqun. Abridged. Vol. 2* (Brooklyn, NY: Darussalam, 2003), 111–2. Shaykh Safiur-Rahman Al-Mubarakpuri, *Tafsir Ibn Kathir: Surat Al-Jathiya to the end of Surat Al-Muunafiqun. Abridged. Vol. 10* (Brooklyn, NY: Darussalam, 2003), 434, 436.

[138] Pim Valkenberg, *World Religions in Dialogue: A Comparative Theological Approach* (Winona, MN: Anselm Academic, 2013), 85. For a confirmation of this observation, see section II in the following citation. *US Department of State. 2019 Report on International Religious Freedom: Jordan. Office of International Religious Freedom.* Retrieved from: https://www.state.gov/reports/2019-report-on-international-religious-freedom/jordan/?msclkid=48856c12ac6c11e-cb7745008b0739c95.

However, as one scrutinizes the Qur'an, two things become apparent; the Qur'an is not founded on the West's ideology despite its evident influence, and significant gaps in historical information appear absent. Moreover, the qur'anic moral standards set by Muhammad seem hypocritical and, at times, appalling considering today's Western standards and those of many Muslim adherents worldwide. Therefore, we must consider the origin and development of the Qur'an.

Origin and Development

Although this researcher briefly mentioned in the section above Muhammad's experience at the cave in Hira, surah 96 technically stands as the first chapter espousing the qur'anic revelation when supposedly the angel Gabriel told him to recite. According to Ibn Sa'd, Muhammad's cousin Ibn Abbas, who allegedly walked with him and was recognized as one of the early faithful companions, never said that Waraqa Ibn Nawfal ever named the angel Gabriel as the source bringing the revelation to Muhammad. Thus, based on the three distinct versions of Muhammad's first encounter in the cave at Hira, Spencer ponders whether Muhammad retold the story differently. However, this researcher wonders if Muhammad's story was a created fable or a figment of the narrator's imagination. Nevertheless, all sources except Jabir ibn Hayyan's agree that surah 96 remains the first revelation.[139]

Unfortunately, the Qur'an begins under problematic logical inconsistencies, which exist as only the beginning of the many issues undermining the validity of the revelation because if it authentically comes from a divine source, then the heavenly informant was less than perfect. The Caner brothers' excellent research on the beginning of Muhammad's revelation (surah 96:1) brings striking evidence that undermines the entirety of the Qur'an as a divine revelation. If Muhammad viewed women as inferior to men, why did he need Khadija to confirm that his experience came from Allah?

---

[139] Spencer, *The History of Jihad*, 94–6.

Furthermore, the Caners point out that Muhammad thought he was possessed and doubted that it came from Allah. Lastly, the Caners highlight that Muhammad thought the angel's message perhaps identified as communication from Jinn or the dead, which sets the ground for a blasphemous origin.[140]

An interesting attempt to reframe surah 96 comes from the Syro-Aramaic translation of the chapter by Christoph Luxenberg because he suggests that its first ayat primarily exists as a call to prayer.[141] However, the problem with Luxenberg's assessment arises when he also indicates that by comparing the usage of similar words and phrases in other passages to those in surah 96:1, "recite" suggests "you will forget nothing."[142] Ironically, this would undermine Muhammad's alleged deific-based inspiration from Allah and writing the Qur'an in the manner that put his plan to conquer and unite the entire Arabian Peninsula forward to aggressively pursue and destroy his theistic opponents in other lands he proposed to subjugate.

The observation above allowed the newly founded Islamic religion to implement the qur'anic chapter of *Al-Tawba* (surah of the sword) and replace many peaceful Meccan surahs written before its creation when Muhammad did not have any military power. In contrast, the ninth chapter of the Qur'an commanded the murder, humiliation, and subjugation of all idolaters, Jews, and Christians who did not believe in Muhammad because they perceived his deific source of inspiration as false. Indeed, one notices the reaffirmation that Qathem or those behind the usurpation of the messianic title of Muhammad (perhaps Muawiya I) used *Naskh* to justify his diabolic agenda against Jews, Christians, and unbelievers. These groups

---

[140] Ergun Mehmet Caner and Emir Fethi Caner, *Unveiling Islam: An Insider's look at Muslim Life and Beliefs*, 40–44. The tafsir of Ibn Kathir shows that women have "half a brain" because, in a court session where one man cannot attend, two women must substitute his place as a witness due to their deficiency of the mind. Shaykh Safiur-Rahman Al-Mubarakpuri, *Tafsir Ibn Kathir: Surat Al-Jathiya to the end of Surat Al-Muunafiqun. Abridged. Vol. 2* (Brooklyn, NY: Darussalam, 2003), 87–9.

[141] Christoph Luxenberg, *The Syro-Aramaic Reading of the Koran*, 302–5.

[142] Ibid., 303.

mentioned were persecuted for their beliefs, not for committing any physical attacks on Muhammad or the following generations of Jews and Christians up to this day. Moreover, the Muslims did not need to worry about their finances because the tafsir explicitly stated they would acquire riches by stealing from the Jews, Christians, and unbelievers through conquest.[143]

Al-Jalalayn, one of the most respected Islamic scholars commenting in his tafsir on the doctrine of abrogation known in Arabic as Naskh, outlined the reasons behind surahs 2:106 and 16:101, explaining Muhammad's motives for replacing former qur'anic texts with "newly" inspired ones. Al-Jalalayn states that many accused him of exchanging ayat to benefit his desired goals.[144] Imam Abul Hussain Muslim ibn Al-Hajjaj shows that when others felt guilty because they forgot the Quran verses, Muhammad said Allah caused them to fail in their recollections of the "holy" words.[145] Moreover, Imam Muslim stated that Ibn Abbas said the Qur'an came under seven different recitations because Muhammad allegedly asked the "angel" Jibril to recite it in seven modes.[146] Indeed, one perceives that Muhammad thought his people incapable of interpreting the Qur'an in one recitation.

The current Islamic reformation efforts by the erudite scholars above targeting the linguistic origins of the Qur'an do not detract from the 270 million lives lost at the behest of Islamic caliphates and leaders who manipulated or interpreted the qur'anic mandates of this semi-mythical figure Muhammad (or Qathem).[147] Although

---

[143] Ibid., Bewley, Bewley, and Waley, *Tafsir Al-Jalalayn*, 404–7, 419, 435.

[144] Bewley, Bewley, and Waley, *Tafsir Al-Jalalayn*, 38, 583.

[145] Hafiz Abu Tahir Zubair "Ali Za'i, Nasiruddin Al-Khattab, and Abu Khaliyl, *English Translation of Sahih Muslim Compiled by: Imam Abul Hussain Muslim Ibn al-Hajjaj. Vol. 2. [1838] 225, [1841] 228 – (790)* (Brooklyn, NY: Darussalam, 2007), 308–11, 336–7.

[146] Za'i et al., *Sahih Muslim. Vol. 2. Hadith 1899–1907*, 334–9.

[147] Roark establishes that 270 million lives were lost through Islamic Jihad over 1,400 years. Dallas M. Roark, *Answering Islam: A Christian-Muslim Dialogue. Is There Jihad in the Old Testament?* Retrieved from: https://answering-islam. org/authors/roark/jihad_ot.html. Warner affirms Roark's findings regarding the deaths of 270 million under Islamic jihad for 1400 years. Bill Warner, *Sharia*

Spencer does not deny or confirm the number of deaths caused by the Qur'an's "divine revelatory mandates, his astute observation lays out that if Muhammad was a creation or not, the Arabic empire's rise by the use of the Qur'an's teachings remains a "matter of record."[148] Moreover, Spencer explains that a reconstruction of qur'anic and hadith stands apparent considering that early writings speak of a somewhat theological kinship between Jews, Christians, and Muslims, suggesting that perhaps the Arabic prophetic figure did not exist as he is currently known.[149]

One of the significantly problematic issues with the Qur'an's development lies in its unmethodical compilation by several sources, which appear somewhat unresolved and inexplicable. On the one hand, the new studies initiated by modern Western scholars like Lüling suggest that Qur'anic scriptures existed before the Islamic narrative's approximal dates of its emergence.[150] Lüling states that the heretical Christian group of Central Arabia, the *Hanif*, held an alleged Christianized Koran in 500 AD, which previously existed one hundred years before the traditionally Islamic Qur'an emerged. This researcher believes that Lüling is not only referring to the Christian heretical and orthodox concepts found in the Qur'an but the actual preexistent writing to the traditional seven (today twenty six) versions of the existent Qur'an used in the Middle East.[151] On the other hand, Muslim scholars show the method in which the Qur'an was inspired, written, and collected, which seems to be the consensus

---

for Non-Muslims: Center for the Study of Political Islam. ISBN 0-9795794-8-1 and ISBN 978-0-9795794-8-6. V 1.23.2017. (USA, CSPI, LLC, 2010), 25. Retrieved from: https://petterssonsblogg.se/wp-content/uploads/2017/05/sharia_law_for_non-muslims.pdf. Moreover, Dakdok numbers the deaths caused by Islamic jihad at a massive five hundred million. However, this author finds Dakdok's numbers doubtful. Dakdok, *Exposing the Truth About Jihad. Vol. 1 of 2*, 345.

[148] Spencer, *Did Muhammad Exist*, 248–52.

[149] Spencer seems to believe that the qur'anic scriptures were manipulated to favor the Arabic empire's rise to power, and Patricia Crone believes Muhammad did exist and impelled its establishment. Ibid., 257–60.

[150] Lüling, *A Challenge to Islam for Reformation*, 339–40.

[151] Ibid.

reached by most modern Muslims despite the Islamic branch many may follow theologically.

In the Sahih ahadith compiled by Imam Muslim, he shows how the Qur'an was collected by some of his companions (four of his closest followers) and then redistributed throughout the Islamically controlled regions of the AP. Imam Muslim shows that the odd and almost fantastical method used to write the allegedly inspired surahs was on the rocks and leaves whenever the so-called prophet Muhammad had a revelation.[152] Most Muslims believe in the Islamic narrative concerning the emergent timing of the Qur'an instead of the newly found discoveries regarding the Jewish and sectarian Christian monotheistic written concepts preexisting in the Arabian Peninsula because their traditional faith remains embedded. Still, this writer remains dubious about the claim of Islamic texts being written on bone and leaves (regardless of the kind) because it becomes almost an insulting fairy tale if artificially fitted during the sixth and seventh centuries. Considering the Arabic exposure to the Hellenized Roman Christianized culture and the Persian Empire in previous centuries, where Arab traders would encounter writings on parchment and scrolls, it seems debatable to believe they could not do the same.[153]

As we have discovered earlier in this thesis, the Nabataeans, Sabeans, and South Arabians would have become familiar with these writing techniques. Thus, one gathers that the trading interactions between northern and southern tribes with the Central Arabic tribal groups would have made these materials and techniques available for writing the Qur'an. Moreover, Muhammad refers to the Jewish and Christian scriptures confirming their existence. This tells us that no logical reasoning exists behind writing qur'anic texts or Muhammad's

---

[152] Muhammad Muhsin Khan, *The Translation of the Meanings of Sahih Al-Bukhari. Arabic-English. Vol. 6. Hadith 4986* (Riyadh, SAE: Darussalam, 2008), 424–6.

[153] The following authors show how the Old and New Testament scrolls existed during the first and second centuries AD Walter C. Kaiser Jr. and Moises Silva, *Introduction to Biblical Hermeneutics: The Search for Meaning. Revised and Expanded Edition* (Grand Rapids, MI: Zondervan, 2011), 117–9. William W. Klein, Craig L. Blomberg, and Robert L. Hubbard, *Introduction to Biblical Interpretation. 3rd Ed* (Grand Rapids, MI: Zondervan, 2017), 187.

sunnah on leaves and rocks.[154] However, the various Qur'an writings and traditions surrounding them tell us that perhaps the truth lies somewhere in the middle because it remains integrated into every sharia discipline followed throughout the Muslim-dominated countries.[155]

Imam Al-Suyuti (849–911 AD) sees that the Qur'an does not necessarily follow a chronological order because the collocation of each surah relies on its length over the contextualization of its content according to its various compilers. Al-Suyuti states that while some scholars believe Muhammad arranged the chapters of the modern Qur'an, others suggest the companions of the Arabian prophet accommodated the qur'anic order. However, they all agree that the Qur'an remains divinely ordered.[156] Still, the problem that follows from this seemingly divine issue is that the traditions evolving from this minor dilemma became the wood for the fire, which later consumed the Muslim world by pitting believers in Muhammad against each other.[157] Notice that the work cited above inadvertently shows the initial reason for disagreements on sharia practices between the Sunnis, Shia, and Sufi (the Sufi come much later than the aforementioned), which Al-Suyuti states, "The companions arranged the suras without knowing about those that were eliminated." Indeed, one can observe some of these problems in the doctrine of mut'a, which Muhammad ordered and never condemned in the Qur'an, but Umar

---

[154] Dakdok affirms the existence of the Old Testament scrolls and the over five thousand copies of the New Testament (see 119), which conclusively leads one to recognize that Qathem most likely referred to these uncorrupted duplicates compiled in the Bibles he encountered despite later saying that Jews and Christians corrupted the writings, probably under the guidance of Waraqa Ibn Nawfal, the rogue priest. Dakdok, *The Generous Qur'an. Surah 3:3–4*, 30.

[155] Al-Suyuti suggests that the Qur'an remains "intertwined" within the Islamic religion itself. Thus, the tafsir scholars needed to discern the more profound meanings expounded by the Qur'an. Adnan Karim and Ayman Khalid, *Secrets Within the Order of the Qur'an: al-Hafiz, al-Mufassir. Jalal al-Din al-Suyuti (d. 911h)* (Birmingham, UK: Dar al-Arqam Publishing, 2018), 16–7.

[156] Ibid., 29–42.

[157] Various Muslim interpreters did not know about previous abrogations done to the Qur'an by Islamic authorities. Ibid., 42.

Khattab did in the hadith compilations.[158] Although the size of the qur'anic chapters makes no difference regarding their placement, the theological and historical content's order of their passages does.

Unlike the Bible's origins, the Qur'an's emergence becomes muddled by the editing of the hadith compilers and the creators of the Islamic tafsirs because they explicitly mention how they came about the information concerning the prophet, which was through hearsay.[159] The teachers of the Tafsirs placed in perspective its theological and historical content two to three hundred years after the Qur'an and some ahadith emerged if the Muslim narratives about Muhammad and his inspiration are authentic. Although Jews and Christians developed commentaries to parse the theological meanings of the Scriptures, they still possessed a solid body of literary works written by the prophets. They could coherently contextualize the purpose of the texts by the logical and historical sequence of the passages within the chapters and books. Unfortunately, Muslims had to figure out what parts of the Qur'an were authentic or false under the direction of chain narrators, who many even considered untrustworthy because the surahs did not follow a sequential order nor the ayat themselves (if one follows the modern Muslim narratives).

Unfortunately, the portion speaking of *Hafs Ibn Sulayman* reads only in Arabic. Still, the story of how many considered him a liar and his hadith narration weak exists in some of the following passages. Imam Muslim shows that many were speaking ahadith considered

---

[158] Al-Hilali and Khan, *Interpretations of The Meanings of The Noble Qur'an in The English Language. Vol. 1. 4:24,* 115. Christian Prince. *Sex & Allah. Vol. I,* 12–3. Momen affirms this researcher's illustration regarding the issue of mut'a between the Sunnis and Shi'a in his investigative literary work on Shi'i Islam. Moojan Momen, *An Introduction to Shi'i Islam* (New Haven, CT: Yale University Press, 1985), 182–3.

[159] As highlighted at the beginning of most of the hadith cited throughout this thesis. Indeed, the previous fact leaves the hadith writers who did not witness or hear anything from Muhammad to discern what sounds true to the traditions passed through previous generations.

"Daif" (weak).[160] The significance of mentioning the Hafs reading of the Qur'an is that it remains the most adhered recitation.

The following section will briefly discuss whether Western inquiries that insinuate reform based on recent discoveries of linguistic variations hold more credibility or if the traditional Islamic narratives maintain more weight theoretically. After all, the Qur'an's ayat without the ahadith collections and tafsirs, in many instances, would become incomprehensible because they do not necessarily follow a consistent chronological or contextual order. Patricia Crone's insightful observation highlights that although the people who were with Muhammad and those immediately after him should have familiarized themselves with the Qur'an's linguistic usage, they seemed lost regarding the significance and interpretation of its passages.[161] Indeed, this caused error and confusion in its traditional consensus. Moreover, Warraq points out that the Koran itself states that some of its texts remain ambiguous because Muhammad himself said that no one knows the interpretation but God.[162] However, the Arabian prophet would not have minded if his followers did not understand his words because he would have become suspicious of their motives if they raised questions about the topics he speaks of.[163]

Al-Jalalayn gives a faulty excuse to Muslim believers for asking about the revelations given to the prophet Muhammad, which seem difficult to interpret. He suggests that believers receive clarity about an ayat if Muhammad remains alive and simultaneously says they will remain ambiguous after his death. Therefore, Muslims should ignore them because Allah has ignored these passages. Indeed, this raises questions concerning the wisdom and omniscience of the Islamic deity Allah because it makes him appear doubleminded.[164]

---

160 Hafiz Abu Tahir Zubair "Ali Za'i, Nasiruddin Al-Khattab, and Abu Khaliyl, *English Translation of Sahih Muslim Compiled by: Imam Abul Hussain Muslim Ibn al-Hajjaj. Vol. 1. 01 to 1160. [15] – 6 (6); [16] 7 – (7); [21]; [85]; [91]* (Brooklyn, NY: Darussalam, 2007), 48–9, 51, 74–8.

161 Warraq, *What the Koran Really Says*, 40–1.

162 Ibid.

163 Usama Dakdok, *The Generous Qur'an. Surah. 5:101*, 75.

164 Bewley, Bewley, and Waley, *Tafsir Al-Jalalayn*, 271.

Still, the issue is that the Qur'an's legitimate origins remain fundamentally compromised historically and theologically, which, to this author, makes it comparably inferior to its Jewish and Christian predecessors' Holy Scriptures. Although the Qur'an remains the primary Islamic book of theological guidance for Muslim believers, the ahadith compilations allegedly consist of Muhammad's sayings under the divine inspiration of his deity Allah. However, if one carefully ponders on this belief highlighted above, it becomes problematic because Allah technically speaks in the Qur'an and the ahadith collections. Ironically, this suggests that other sources after the Quran's revelation have the authority to invalidate some of its mandates, as observed when Umar Khattab abolished the practice of mut'a (qur'anic legalized prostitution), whereas Muhammad endorsed it. In contrast, Allah never did, according to Muhammad (see citation 157). Indeed, according to its textual content, the Qur'an appears more like a "glorified hadith" that Muslims must primarily follow over all other hadith despite both containing the sayings of Muhammad under Allah's inspiration.[165]

Thus, the doctrine of abrogation (*Naskh*) undermines the whole belief system of Islam right from its inception. Ironically, to say that when a hadith contradicts the Qur'an, its rejection stands imminent because it conflicts with Allah's "divine inspiration" proves itself a theoretical oxymoron. After all, the Islamic scholar Al-Jalalayn says that the Qur'an does not identify as a narrative but a confirmation of all the holy Abrahamic books before it.[166] However, this causes a conflict when many beliefs practiced by Muslims are not found in its pages but the ahadith compilations.[167] Indeed, this muddles the origins of Islamic traditions practiced by the Muslim populace and causes theological confusion because it directly undermines the word of Allah if one must wonder whether the deity mandated any specific

---

[165] Usama Dakdok, *The Generous Qur'an 39:23,* 267.

[166] Al-Jalalayn comments on surah 12:111 that it remains the final narrative. Bewley, Bewley, and Waley., *Tafsir Al-Jalalayn,* 519.

[167] Za'i, Al-Khattab, and Khaliyl., *Sahih Muslim Vol. 2. [1284] 93; [1379] 166-(610); [1380] 167,* 68, 108–9.

ritual or the man Qathem and his companions enacted them.[168] The most embarrassing fact about the qur'anic origins lies in the opinion of those who allegedly lived during the time of Qathem and immediately caught on to his false inspirations when he continually changed the supposed words of Allah for other more convenient mandates.[169]

After investigating the facts surrounding the origins of the Qur'an's writings, they appear to include Christological material found within its pages. Did Qathem learn this from Waraqa Ibn Nawfal, the Jewish monotheists, the sectarian Christians trading throughout the Arabian Peninsula (AP), or those living amongst the Central Arabic tribes? Previously, the influence of Waraqa Ibn Nawfal was discussed in the sections above (see footnotes 110–112, 121). However, according to Ibn Ishaq cited above, one should note that Waraqa Ibn Nawfal had to "teach" Muhammad that his alleged angelic encounter was with *Jibril* (Gabriel). This would theoretically suggest that the Arabian prophet knew nothing about the Abrahamic God nor any of his heavenly hosts described by the preceding Holy Scriptures of the Jewish people and the Christians.

Considering the observation above, it would technically dismiss the "*Hannifin*" theory regarding Abraham because it implies Qathem was more of an opportunist familiarized with some of the surrounding religions but committed to none theologically.[170] Moreover, surah 3:118 comes after the Jewish people of Medina begin reject-

---

[168] Ironically, Muhammad admits that some of the ayat he forgot by human fault; others reminded him of them. Still, others were forgotten by divine causation, which makes the entirety of the Qur'an a religious fable or at least a plagiarized version of the preceding religious books (the Jewish and Christian Scriptures) and old fictitious Arabian tales. Ibid., *[1838–43]*, 308–10.

[169] One observes that Muhammad (Qathem) excuses himself from the forgeries by suggesting that the people did not understand the convenience of abrogation (surah. 16:101). Bewley, Bewley, and Waley., *Tafsir Al-Jalalayn*, 583.

[170] Describing Abraham as *Hanif* becomes a strange but convenient way for Muhammad to hitch his Arabic monotheistic or henotheistic concepts to Abrahamic monotheism. Bukhari details the theological idea of *Hanif*. Khan, *Sahih Al-Bukhari Vol. 5. Hadith* 3827, 101–2. Again, if Muhammad had learned anything from the *Hanif* monotheistic cult of Central Arabia, it would still have been identified as a paganized theistic belief.

ing Muhammad because of his theological inconsistencies with their Holy Scriptures, which also cost Muhammad the military loss of the Jews' support against Mecca.[171] Additionally, Muhammad desired to purposely distinguish himself from the Jews when one pointed out that he stood up during a funeral procession like those following Judaic rites, so he told the Muslims to sit once they passed. Nevertheless, Muhammad wanted to impose on the Jewish people his false prophethood when they rejected him by calling him a liar.[172] The primary point of the previous observations revealing his dealings with the Jewish people remains significant because it suggests that despite Muhammad coming to learn authentic Abrahamic monotheism in Medina, he ultimately rejected its prophetic criteria, which identified him as categorically false. After all, surah 10:94–5 tells its readers that Muhammad was not illiterate as the modern Muslim narratives proclaim.[173]

Secondly, the language of the Qur'an does not consist of a pure classical Arabic script but Syro-Aramaic corruptions of sorts, which shows that perhaps it did not come together over twenty-three years as the Islamic tradition suggests but from sporadic periods much earlier, during, and after Qathem's lifetime.[174] Equating the creation of the Qur'an to the order in which the Old and New Testament scriptures were created and canonized by attempting to reform its overall Islamic focus through intentional textual eisegesis appears challenging and almost fallacious. Undoubtedly, the Qur'an's origins

---

[171] Guillaume, *The Life of Muhammad*, 262–3. The Caner brothers confirm Ibn Ishaq's narrative in Guillaume's interpretation. Caner and Caner, *Unveiling Islam*, 46. Notice that Bewley et al. affirm Ibn Ishaq's assessment of the situation cited by Guillaume when they equate the "rejection" of Muhammad's prophethood with "hate," and the Arabian prophet suggests "departing from them," meaning the Jews. Bewley, Bewley, and Waley, *Tafsir Al-Jalalayn*, 148. Dakdok, *The Generous Qur'an. Surah 3:118*, 40.

[172] Khan, *Sahih Al-Bukhari Vol. 5. Hadith 3911*, 154–7.

[173] Dakdok, *The Generous Qur'an. Surah 10-94-5*, 129.

[174] Luxenberg, *The Syro-Aramaic Reading of the Qur'an*, 10–1. Warraq states that despite the Qur'an's assertions of being written in plain Arabic, it contains many unfamiliar words to the language, which remain nebulous because they appear to have morphed from another. Warraq, *What the Koran Really Says*, 38–9.

appear structured as a rejection of a possible minority of Trinitarian Christians that resided in the AP and the Jewish people's "chosen" status, referring to both groups as "people of the book" while villainizing their theological motives and filial connections to their counterparts in the AP. Ibn Kathir's comments on surah 3:110 show how Muhammad villainizes the Jews and Christians by suggesting that his Ummah were the best of peoples.[175]

Thus, despite the information presented in most of the sections above showing Judaic and Christian influences within the pages of the Qur'an, its final literary form appears to have come from forces that desired to intentionally distinguish its message from those in the preceding holy books.[176] Indeed, the observation above affirms Islam's emergence as ultimately being a politically driven agenda, which incidentally can only do so by claiming divine status through the "inspired" Qur'an and its prophet. Hence, this author will seek to briefly demonstrate these observations in the section below while moving on to other relevant topics.

---

[175] Oddly, the so-called Arabian prophet says his people are the best because they bring the preceding groups with chains around their necks in submission. Shaykh Safiur-Rahman Al-Mubarakpuri. *Tafsir Ibn Kathir: Surat Al-Baqarah, Verse 253 to Surat An-Nisa, Verse 147. To the end of Surat Al-Muunafiqun. Abridged. Vol. 2* (Brooklyn, NY: Darussalam, 2003), 237–9.

[176] Ibn Kathir shows the Islamic scholars At-Tirmidhi, Ibn Majah, and Al-Hakim stating that Muhammad was given the "perfect" and "complete" law never handed to any before him, meaning the Old or New Testament prophets. Indeed, this makes Muhammad the "seal of the prophets," and thus, the Qur'an is Allah's final revelation. Ibid., 238–9.

Religious Beliefs and Practices

Superficially, Islam lines up with Judaism and Christianity in its practices resembling the outward beliefs of the latter two faiths. Like its predecessors, Islam today is indeed a monotheistic religion.[177] Halverson outlines Islam's similarities with its predecessor, Christianity, by showing their superficial theological beliefs in God, angels, prophets, holy books, and the final judgment.[178] Additionally, Halverson explains Islamic religious practices like prayer, fasting, alms, and the *shahada* by comparing the procedures that differ substantially in one way or another.[179] There is nothing unique about the *shahada* (declaration of belief in Allah and Muhammad) in that other religions claim exclusivity concerning the legitimacy of their deities, prophets, and inspirations as the way to attaining divine truths.

This confession resembles the Jewish or Christian monotheistic creeds (i.e., the Israeli *Shema* in Deuteronomy 6:4 states "the Lord is One" or the Nicene Creed of AD 325, which remains the only ecumenical statement confessed by most Christians concerning God's Divine Triunity). However, the exception lies in the association of Muhammad with Allah to attain the opportunity of salvation despite the Arabian prophet's sinful condition and mortality, lacking a deific divinity. Ironically, the Arabian prophet condemns Christians for

---

[177] Luling, *A Challenge to Islam for Reformation*, 340–1. Dean Halverson, *The Illustrated Guide to World Religions* (Bloomington, MN: Bethany House Publishers, 2003), 107–11.

[178] Ibid., Dean Halverson.

[179] Ibid.

associating a partner with Allah yet makes himself equally significant to his deity and necessary for salvation.[180]

However, as one delves deeper into the procedural rites accompanying these religious practices, the theological differences between the Jewish, Christian, and Islamic religions widen and become apparent and undeniable. In the Islamic religion, prayer is one of its "seven pillars of faith," which requires several rites that may resemble Judaism due to its legalistic approach to serving Allah but lacks its Christian predecessor's concept of divine grace regarding salvation. Bukhari outlines six pillars of Islam, which include faith in Allah and his messenger (shahada), *Zakat* (alms), *Salat* (prayer), *Saum* (fasting), *Hajj* (pilgrimage), and *Jihad* ("holy fighting"). Muhammad said Jihad stands as one of the pillars of faith, and he desired a life of repeated martyrdom in the service of Allah.[181] Momen affirms the observation above by stating that jihad for the Shi'a is a mandatory duty for every Muslim, but only imams can order its enactment.[182]

Prayer

Generally, prayer in most religions is the vehicle of communication to any specific deity(s) of religious adherents who desire to acquire favor, aid, or strength to live piously. Muhammad changed the direction of prayer and abrogated verses to freely shape this custom without being theologically challenged by the Jewish believers that knew their scriptures and could use this against his false prophethood. Noticeably, the direction of prayer (*Salat*) and the procedures and practices associated with it found in the Qur'an, ahadith compi-

---

[180] Dakdok, *The Generous Qur'an. Surah. 3:32; 4:48, 116; 9:29*, 33, 53, 59, 114. The apostle John presents Jesus as the *logos*, and Yeshua HaMashiach explicitly makes Himself equal to God when He identified as the Divine Son. Lockman, *Jn. 1:1–3; 5:19–30*, 1812, 1826–7.

[181] Ibid., Ch. 26, 40–2. Hadith. 36, 50, 53–4, 57, 72–3, 81, 83–7. Muhammad Muhsin Khan, *The Translation of The Meanings of Sahih Al-Bukhari. Arabic to English. Vol. 9. Ahadith 6861 to 7563. Hadith. 7226–7* (Riyadh, SAE: Darussalam, 2008), 210.

[182] Moojan Momen, *An Introduction to Shi'i Islam*, 180.

lations, and tafsirs seem exclusively shaped by Muhammad and Umar bin Al-Khattab while excluding Allah's contributions to the establishment of this pillar. Umar asserts that he "invoked" three things practiced by believers today regarding the Islamic pillars of faith that he desired Muhammad to change. Thus, the prophet complied when he changed the direction and place of the prayers.[183]

The resemblance between Islamic and Jewish ritualistic prayers lies in the Qur'an surahs 2:238 and 11:114, demanding prayer devotions from Allah's adherents three times daily. The Bible shows the prophet Daniel praying three times daily, suggesting that this was a Jewish custom, perhaps much earlier than the Babylonian captivity.[184] Moreover, the Bible indicates in Solomon's dedication to the temple that Jewish believers prayed toward it in reverence to the Living God, *Yahweh-Elohim*, establishing the direction of prayers that the Jewish people would traditionally communicate with God.[185]

Similarly, Muslims today pray toward Mecca. However, Muhammad prayed toward Jerusalem in Medina while still attempting to convince the Jews of his prophethood (shown in the citations of Bukhari). In contrast, the hadith compilations contradict the "prayer quota" of Jewish beliefs because they require praying five times a day, according to the hadith.[186] The prior comparisons show the similarities between Jews and Muslims despite the differences in rituals and preparations. Nevertheless, as mentioned earlier, most of the peoples of the AP before Islam, apart from the Jewish people, prayed toward Petra as most of the ancient Qiblas indicated (see pg. 10 on Gibson's findings).

---

[183] Safiur-Rahman and Al-Mubarakpuri, *Tafsir Ibn Kathir. Vol. 1*, 434–7. Muhammad Muhsin Khan, *The Translation of the Meanings of Sahih Al-Bukhari. Arabic-English. Vol. 1. Ahadith 001 to 875. Book 4. Ch. 1, Hadith. 395–9, 402–3* (Riyadh, SAE: Darussalam, 2008) 135, 261–5. The practice of Wudu (ablution) must occur before Muslims can offer Salat (prayer).

[184] Lockman, *Dan. 6:10–1*, 1436.

[185] Ibid., *1 Kgs. 8:28–36*, 567.

[186] Za'i et al., *Sahih Muslim. Vol. 2. Hadith 1379–80, 1522*, 108–9, 172.

Dawah

Dawah is the vehicle of "invitation" to Islam by presenting the words of Muhammad and his deity Allah as the Christians' evangelization method of outreach to the masses by introducing the wonderous salvific plan and works of Jesus Christ. However, Muhammad and his followers performed dawah by stating that people's property and lives were safe if they accepted Muhammad and his deity Allah. Otherwise, if they did not take Allah and his self-proclaimed prophet, the results always included rape, pillaging, and murder.[187] In the West, Dawah remains a docile practice of inviting people to believe in Allah and his messenger due to Islam's current governmental, military, and weak public influence on the societal structure.

The Paganism in Hajj

Although one can continue making contrasts and comparisons between Islam and its Abrahamic predecessors, it seems more time-efficient to look at a few of the religious rituals that originated through a mixture of ancient paganized Arabic beliefs embedded in its modern practice. For example, Kathir shows how the Islamic tradition performed by passing between As-Safa and Al-Marwa began with Hagar's frantic search for water, which replaced the previous cultic practice by the pagan Arabs, which stands identical to today's Muslim tradition.[188] Moreover, in the Islamic tradition of Hajj, several pagan components are hailed as holy and essential in their theology.[189] One of these religious requirements entails circling the Kaaba seven times (*tawaf*), which Abraham, the progenitor of the Arabs, allegedly built out of appreciation for Allah's provision of a ram's substitution for

---

[187] Dakdok, *Exposing the Truth About the Qur'an. Vol. 2 of 2*, 313, 339–40.

[188] Safiur-Rahman and Al-Mubarakpuri, *Tafsir Ibn Kathir. Vol. 1*, 388–9. Caner and Caner, *Unveiling Islam*, 129.

[189] Gibson shows that Hajj stems from an ancient Nabataean cultic practice honoring the dead and deifying leaders. Gibson, *The Nabataeans*, 191–2. Dakdok, *The Generous Qur'an. 2:158*, 15–6.

Ismael, although this event never occurred.[190] Furthermore, Bukhari shows the fictitious circumstances that led Abraham and Ismael to allegedly construct the Kaaba, although ironically highlighting that Ismael was not the father of the Arabian peoples because the tribe of Jurhum (Arabs "desert dwellers") taught him Arabic (as stated earlier, Ismaelites did not consider themselves Arabic).[191] Ibn Kathir affirms Bukhari's assessment concerning the tribe of Jurhum teaching Ismael the Arabic language, which explicitly confirms that the Central Arab origins of the Meccans lie elsewhere.

Ironically, the Islamic practice of Hajj (pilgrimage), which entails circling the black stone considered a holy relic within the Kaaba, was established while the pagan Arabs still performed the ritual.[192] Make no mistake in confusing the biblical story that presents circling the walls of Jericho with being the origin of going around the Kaaba and kissing the black stone.[193] The ancient practice remains a refaced pagan ritual still showing itself problematic to many believing Muslim women who perform Hajj amidst numerous crowds of Muslim men swirling around the Kaaba and the black stone. Ali shows how modern Muslim men continue to grope and sexually assault believing Muslim women who jointly perform the Hajj with them.[194] Nevertheless, because these groups reside in an Islamic country while performing the Hajj, the act is considered a common factor and usually goes unpunished by the authorities.

Nevertheless, the usurper(s) of the Christ-title Muhammad incorporated circling the Kaaba with clothing because of a specific woman Qathem (or another) desired for himself, who walked naked around the Kaaba and black stone, which he did not want anyone

---

[190] The Caner brothers explain the modern Muslim practice and rituals of Hajj. Caner and Caner, *Unveiling Islam*, 128–30, 154–5.

[191] Khan, *Sahih Al-Bukhari Vol. 4. Hadith. 3364*, 351–6.

[192] Wissam Youssif, *Islam in Christ's Eyes: A Scriptural Study on the Origins of Islam and the Christian Response* (Middletown, DE: ACM, 2021), 65. Khan, *Sahih Al-Bukhari. Vol. 2. Hadith. 1643*, 405–7.

[193] Lockman, Josh. 6:3–10, 15–6, 20, 346. Khan, *Sahih Al-Bukhari Vol. 2. Hadith. 1597, 1609–15*, 385, 390–2.

[194] Ayaan Hirsi Ali, *Prey: Immigration, Islam, and the Erosion of Women's Rights* (New York, NY: Harper-Collins, 2021), 153.

else to look upon her nakedness.[195] Indeed, walking around the Kaaba has nothing to do with any traditions related to the Jewish and Christian God. However, walking around the Kaaba and kissing the black stone began under a pagan fertilization ritual dedicated to the gods of the desert.[196] Most likely, the early Meccan women and most across the AP would pray to the gods, including Allah, and touch themselves and extract the blood from their private parts to spread it on the black stone to become fertile (see footnote Prince, 195–196). Thus, the practice of Hajj comes from the AP1's ancient idolatrous and henotheistic worship involving blood sacrifice and sexualized rituals that historically identified with the ANE world from where *Yahweh* revealed Himself to the Hebrew patriarchs and created a theologically distinct people by displaying His power.[197]

Hence, one realizes that Israel received the Mosaic laws after God's miraculous display of glorious power over all fictitious gods, anchoring Jewish traditions in the reality of those events depicted in the Holy Scriptures. Block points out that the Israelites' God, *Yahweh*, in contrast to all other nations during their early stages, was a responsive deity who caused significant changes and validated their religious beliefs in Him, unlike those of the surrounding peoples.[198] In contrast, this author suggests that Islam's theological origins started as an assortment of Arab monotheistic beliefs resembling henotheism, reinforced by Jewish monotheism and the Monophysite Christology. Indeed, all the previous groups denied the deity of Christ. Islam does not stand as a sister Abrahamic religion but exists as a Judaeo-Christian cult. This thesis shows that perhaps monotheism existed in the Arab community during its inception. Still, it immediately devolved into polytheistic religious worship before the divine revelation given to the Jewish people during the Mosaic era, maintaining a

---

[195] Safiur-Rahman and Al-Mubarakpuri, *Tafsir Ibn Kathir. Vol. 7*, 67–74. Bewley et al., *Tafsir Al-Jalalayn*, 755–57. Prince, *Sex and Allah. Vol. 2*, 40–4.

[196] Ibid., Prince.

[197] Archer, *A Survey of Old Testament*, 141–2, 247.

[198] Block, *The Gods of the Nations*, 70–3.

heavy presence until the Umayyad and Abbasid caliphates when an Arab ethnos was needed.[199]

The Hajj example is just one of the few cultic practices that today's Islamic religion espouses as part of an Abrahamic monotheistic tradition related to a religious salvific duty.[200] Indeed, no Judaic or Christian monotheistic tradition affirms this or several other Islamic customs that Muslims believe and practice today as a theologically sound religious ritual related to monotheism. For example, the same black stone used as a vital part of performing Hajj for fertility or other types of cultic worship during the alleged time of Jahiliya will also become part of the judgment against those of the Muslim faith.[201] One of the most ancient and respected Islamic scholars, Jami' At-Tirmidhi, states that the previously mentioned belief comes from the Islamic notion that the black stone at the Kaaba was once white until it became black because of the Arabic peoples' sins.[202] Thus, the Arab pagans, like the seventh-century Muslims and today's followers of Muhammad's Islamic faith, believe that the black stone has the power to cleanse all the sins of every believer that touches it while performing the Hajj.

Indubitably, the black stone presents theological inconsistencies with the monotheistic traditions of the Jewish and Christian believers preceding the Muhammadan view of the forgiveness and eradication of sins within the Islamic faith because it has no Judaeo-Christian scriptural origins. Ibn Juraij said that when Ibn Hisham forbade Muslim women from performing *Tawaf* (circling the Kaaba), they asked Aisha to allow them to touch the black stone, which Al-Bukhari shows that they disguised themselves and committed the act of worship with the men of the locality.[203] Additionally, when a woman told Muhammad that she was sick, he told her to perform Tawaf, which suggests that, like the Arabian prophet, she believed

---

[199] Webb, *Imagining the Arabs*, 95, 130, 264–9.
[200] Macintosh-Smith, 52.
[201] Prince, *El Engaño de Allah*, 108–9.
[202] Ibid., 109.
[203] Khan, *Sahih Al-Bukhari. Vol. 2. 1618–9*, 393–4.

that the black stone provided divine healing.[204] Furthermore, performing Hajj around the black stone was so "sacred" that when the companions of Muhammad pointed out that they were discharging semen from their sexual organs, he suggested the rituals' completion. Notice that despite their state of *ihram*, a ritualistic purification symbolized by bodily washing and a specific attire, he required the completion of the ritual and legalized sexual intercourse.[205] Thus, it does not sound far-fetched to perceive that many pagans kept performing Hajj naked in Muhammad's and his followers' presence until the revelation of *Al-Tawba* (chapter of the sword), when no non-Muslim could no longer participate in the ritual in Mecca (see footnote 188–199, 190–193).

The examples above show that the Meccan belief regarding the sacred role of the black stone at the Kaaba remains unique to the polytheistic religions of the Arabic peoples, later incorporated into the Islamic concept of monotheistic worship. A more profound investigation into the origins of this Muslim veneration of the black stone reveals eerily similar paganistic worship of rocks identical to the Nabataeans. The Nabataean people enhanced stones by either carving human features onto them or considering them sacred because they fell from the sky (meteorites).[206] Thus, the deific similarities between the Nabataeans and the Muslims regarding the role of holy stones shown above by Gibson, Prince, and Khan explicitly reveal that the black stone in Islam has its origins in Arab paganism veering away from Jewish or Christian monotheistic fundamental beliefs.

God and the Angelic Beings

This author believes that, like most cults claiming the main views of a major world religion, Islam allegedly identifies with many fundamental Jewish and Christian theologies while distorting them by redefining their theological significance and characteristics.

---

[204] Ibid.

[205] Corduan, *Neighboring Faiths*, 124. Khan, *Sahih Al-Bukhari. Vol. 9. Hadith 7367*, 280–1.

[206] Gibson, *The Nabataeans*, 166–8.

Although this thesis remains limited to showing the origins of the religion, founder, and practices of the Muslim faith, it seems worth briefly using examples of its alleged common beliefs in God, angels, prophets, holy books, and the final judgment to show the origins of Islam's theological distortions. Still, using the name of Allah across the "Abrahamic spectrum" because of its middle Aramaic roots seems theologically chaotic and incompatible due to the contradictory moral characteristics of the Islamic deity with the Jewish or Christian concepts of God. Indeed, a brief explanation of the statement above will immediately shed light on the Islamic version of Allah. Findings concerning Islam's religious origins may surprise many sincere Muslim believers who consider themselves "Qur'an only" or "Messianic Muslims" with unexpected results because they follow Allah much more closely than his prophet Muhammad.[207] However, this author seeks to show that the origins of Islam maintain a complicated assortment of Jewish, Christian, and pagan beliefs about God, supernatural beings, creation, and many other human issues highlighted in its revered writings.

Glancing over the Qur'an, one finds the name of Allah mentioned numerous times, directly teaching the Arabic reader about the moral and divine qualities of the Islamic deity. Still, deific titles like "*Rabb Alameen*," meaning "Lord Creator," suggests that all created things remain subordinate to Allah.[208] Ironically, Warraq highlights that this title challenges the authority of Allah as an almighty entity when another ayat insinuates otherwise by making his creatures appear insubordinate to his power and seemingly like gods within their right.[209] Warraq seems to believe that the issue above comes from the fact that some ayat were initially Christian verses that Islamic authorities altered for the cause of Arabizing the newly established religion of Islam. Although "pure monotheism" seems the goal

---

[207] The Caner brothers show the primary beliefs of the Messianic Muslims, which outline their belief in Jesus as the Messiah and part of the divine Triunity (like "Jews for Jesus") and continue to refer to God under the name Allah. Caner and Caner, *Unveiling Islam*, 107–8.

[208] Dakdok, *The Generous Qur'an. Surah 1:1*, 1, 371, 376.

[209] Warraq, *What the Koran Really Says*, 147–8.

of the caliphates under the banner of the Arabian figure Muhammad, qur'anic texts like those presented by Warraq and others contest the fact.

This thesis argues that one of the most significant issues in proclaiming Abrahamic monotheistic authenticity and lineage does not stem from the racial or ethnic ties of the Jewish and Arab peoples but from the theological perspective tied to the names of God because these define His moral and divine characteristics. As scholars and former Muslims, the Caner brothers affirm this researcher's views by arguing that using Allah's name by a large swath of Middle Eastern Christians misleadingly denotes God's personality by connoting a purely Islamic idea of God, negatively changing the relationship with His creation.[210] Although some suggest that Allah remains an Arabic variation of the generic title "*Eloh*" or "*Eloah*," the Caners believe that a closer look at the language shows us that the Islamic understanding of the formerly mentioned epithet is not a titulary debate but that of God's proper name (see footnote 65).[211] Thus, aside from the etymological roots of "Al-lah" and "Elohim" and the divine qualities attributed to the Islamic deity overlapping those of the Jewish and Christian God, the morality behind the execution of the judgments on humanity by these deific figures differs significantly.[212] Indeed, the previous observation becomes apparent by the actions of their holy prophets condoned by these deities and the historical, miraculous interactions recorded between their chosen peoples and themselves. Indeed, the Qur'an's assessment of Allah remains an incomplete written work full of confusion concerning this deity's moral standing and

---

[210] Read the entirety of the Caners' arguments for the Christian significance of using God's proper name Yahweh concerning His creation and the anti-Trinitarian implications of replacing Him with Allah. Caner and Caner, *Unveiling Islam*, 104–7.

[211] Caner states that many Middle Eastern Christians who are former Muslims use the Persian term for God, *Khudu*, to avoid confusion. They vehemently disagree with the usage of Allah to describe the biblical God. Ibid. 107.

[212] Youssif argues in favor of identifying Allah as the biblical God, although he explicitly highlights that the qur'anic version of Allah does remain entirely another being. Youssif, *Islam in Christ's Eyes, 23*, 85–91.

mandates, which explicitly expresses to this author that the Qur'anic divinity does not identify with the Jewish and Christian God.[213]

The Islamic belief in angels overlaps with Jewish and Christian teachings regarding their functions that favor the aid of those believers remaining faithful to their God but strays into old mythical tales regarding the creation of these powerful beings and their role in the world.[214] Although Judaism, Christianity, and Islam have a common systematic angelology, the origins depicted by the Islamic sources show significant distinctions that remain foreign to the mainstream or orthodox Jewish and Christian faith. For example, Warraq highlights Guillaume's observation that the Islamic narrative embedded in the Qur'an and hadith as doctrinal does not derive from conventional Jewish sources because they believed God made men lesser than angels.[215] The conceptual roots of angelic beings in the Islamic religion derive from pagan Arab myths and ancient Jewish fables. Indubitably, Judaizers and sectarian Christians had a hand in forming Islamic angelology by dwelling among the Arab people and, more importantly, Muhammad and his followers.[216] This brief discussion will make sharp contrasts and comparisons concerning the origins of angels in the great Abrahamic religions' theological perspectives, which stand nonnegotiable beliefs for each theistic system.

The Second Temple Period (STP), known by others as the intertestamental period, had shaped much of the previous two centuries before the arrival of Jesus Christ in Jerusalem, during His ministry, and after His death and resurrection throughout the lives of the

---

[213] In the following surahs, the Qur'an testifies against the omniscience, immutability, and morality of Allah by showing him consistently contradicting himself and appearing dishonest. Dakdok, *General Qur'an. Surah. 2:106; 3:7, 28, 54–5; 4:142; 5:101; 7:53; 10:64; 16:101*, 11, 30, 35, 61, 75, 94, 127, 162.

[214] Corduan, *Neighboring Faiths*, 114–5.

[215] Warraq, *What the Koran Really Says*, 288, 294.

[216] The following Surah shows that Muhammad was influenced by the Jewish and Christian Scriptures by referring to their writings. Robert Spencer, *The Critical Qur'an: Explained from Key Islamic Commentaries and Contemporary Historical Research. Surah. 3:3; 5:68* (New York, NY: Bombardier, 2021), 44, 91.

Apostles and their later disciples.[217] Thus, Second Temple Judaism influenced the formation of Christian angelology, which mostly came from biblical and pseudepigraphic sources known as apocalyptic writings.[218] These apocalyptic writings attempted to make sense of Jewish suffering by trying to understand the ultimate purpose of God's redemptive plan for Israel and the role of the surrounding Gentile world.[219] Nonetheless, first-century Christians relied heavily on the Old Testament (OT) canon, which existed much earlier. However, other Jewish writings external to the OT, like Ecclesiasticus, were valued but considered a late composure unworthy of canonization.[220] Hence, Christianity's angelology mainly establishes itself on the soundness of the OT scriptures, which provide glimpses of the angelic presence and roles in heaven and on earth that concern the welfare of humanity by carrying out missions fulfilling God's ultimate purpose.[221]

Although Christians do not fully understand God's innate reasoning behind the creation of angels, they have an outlined angelology from the biblical texts describing them as metaphysical beings that are holy and superior to humanity in intellect and might, which ultimately please God by fulfilling missions benefitting humankind.[222] However, following Islamic texts (Qur'an, ahadith, and tafsir) describing angelic beings, it becomes immediately apparent

---

[217] Michael S. Heiser, *Reversing Hermon: Enoch, the Watchers, and the Forgotten Mission of Jesus Christ* (Crane, MO: Defender Publishing, 2017), 1–2, 4, 9.

[218] On the first two pages (143–4), Steyn explains the influence of Jewish angelology on Christianity. Steyn, Gert J. "Hebrews' angelology in the light of early Jewish apocalyptic imagery." *Journal of Early Christian History* 1, no. 1 (2011): 143–164. Retrieved from: https://repository.up.ac.za/bitstream/handle/2263/19974/Steyn_Hebrews(2011).pdf?sequence=1.

[219] Klein et al., *Introduction to Biblical Interpretation*, 562–3.

[220] Judaic scholars believed that God stopped inspiring Old Testament texts five to six hundred years before they compiled the Scriptures. Ibid., 166–71.

[221] These following passages in the OT define some aspects of the nature and roles of angelic beings in God's service. Lockman, *Gen. 28:12–7; Josh. 5:13–5; 2 Kgs. 6:15–8; 19:35; Dan. 10:5–14, 20–1*, 60, 345, 619–20, 649, 144.

[222] Pearlman outlines all that entails the nature of angels according to the Christian faith. Myer Pearlman, *Teologia Biblica y Sistematica. [English Version, Knowing the Doctrines of the Bible]* (Miami, FL: Editorial Vida, 1992), 57–68.

that the primary author(s) reciting or writing about the nature and function of angels was primarily influenced by the stories from the book of Jewish legends. Indeed, this observation makes sense, considering that many sectarian Christians in the Arabian Peninsula did not think of Jesus Christ as God but as a divine creation that stands above all of God's creatures who appeared in human form on earth for the redemption of humanity. This author argues that the previous five hundred years of Judaizers and sectarian Christians played an enormous role in infusing myths and legends into Islamic angelology. The following comparisons will provide much-needed clarity on this issue above.

Unlike the angelic duties listed in orthodox or mainstream Christian angelology, Islamic theology teaches that angels help create human beings, a myth coming directly from the Jewish book of legends, which states that angels participate.[223] In contrast, Christians believe God established a "natural order" for Adam and Eve to reproduce human beings, which has nothing to do with any angelic intervention.[224] Although Judaic myths and Islamic angelology vary slightly on the creation of celestial beings, both agree on fire and water's role in making these entities.[225] Bialik et al. state that angels are made of fire but declare that the archangel Michael identifies as the prince of snow and Gabriel of fire and do not extinguish each other.[226]

---

[223] Hayim Nahman Bialik, Yehoshua Hana Ravnitzky, and William G. Braude, *The Book of Legends Sefer Ha-Aggadah: Legends from the Talmud and Midrash*, *547:112–3; 575:6–7* (New York, NY: Schocken Books, 1992), 575–6. Khan, *Sahih Al-Bukhari Vol. 4. Hadith 3208*, 276.

[224] Lockman, *Gen. 1:27–8*, 7.

[225] Bialik et al., *The Book of Legends*, 513:74, 77, 513–4. Bewley et al., *Tafsir Al-Jalalayn.* 38:75–6. Safiur-Rahman and Al-Mubarakpuri, *Tafsir Ibn Kathir. Vol. 8*, 351–2. Dakdok, *The Generous Qur'an. Surah. 15:27; 21:30; 55:15*, 153, 189, 308. Ironically, Allah will send man and jinn to the eternal fire (surah 55:33–5).

[226] Ibid., Bialik et al. Again, the hadith contradicts the Qur'an by stating that the Angels were made from light instead of water or fire. Safiur-Rahman and Al-Mubarakpuri, *Tafsir Ibn Kathir. Vol. 9*, 382.

Similarly, the Qur'an's author's constant confusion relays that all living things are made of water but the Jinn of fire, which raises the question of whether water applies to the Jinn or not.[227] The canonical OT reflected the Jewish experience, revelation, and beliefs regarding the description of divine beings and their roles in the metaphysical realm of Israel and the world that was passed on to the Christian faith. Still, this researcher argues that Islamic angelology aligns with Jewish mythology and some modern Judaic concepts about angelic beings in the human form than Christianity's hierarchical view outlining the duties and functions of angels.[228] The illustrious Syrian Monophysite Christian, pseudo-Dionysius the Areopagite, eloquently outlined angelic hierarchies, authoritative processes, and administrative capabilities applied to God and humanity within the two former categorical depictions (see footnote 214, 220). Ironically, given the information in the former three passages above, one would think that the Islamic belief in divine beings, Islam, would maintain a similar view.

In the Jewish and Christian worldviews, most believe fallen angels are demonic beings. However, for Islam, the Jinn, whose leader identifies as Iblis (Shaitan), do not exist as angelic beings of origin like in the biblical scriptures (see footnotes 214). Even stranger, the Jinn state that they not only believe in Muhammad's salvific message, but they can attain salvation by affirming that Allah is their Lord, which raises two questions.[229] One, are Jinn eternal, and if not, when were they created? The answer lies in the ahadith and, once again, Jewish myths. Although not precisely the same, Jewish mythologies suggest that the angels were made on the second day of

---

[227] Ibid., Safiur-Rahman, and Al-Mubarakpuri, *Tafsir Ibn Kathir. Vol. 9*, 182 Dakdok, *The Generous Qur'an. Surah 21:30*, 189.

[228] Although Prager makes distinctions between divine and human messengers, he tends to lean toward a consistent physicality concerning the encounters between men and angelic beings. Dennis Prager, *The Rational Bible. Genesis: God, Creation, and Destruction. JPS Translation. Alperson Edition* (Washington, DC: Regnery Faith, 2019), 331, 381–2. Colm Luibheid et al., *Pseudo-Dionysius: The Complete Works* (Mahwah, NJ: Paulist Press, 1987), 159–75.

[229] Bewley et al., *Tafsir Al-Jalalayn*, 1253–55. Za'i et al., *Sahih Muslim Vol. 3. Hadith [7554] 28-(3030), [7557] 30*, 434–5.

creation.[230] The ahadith indicate the Jinn began to exist two thousand years before humanity's appearance on earth.[231] In contrast, neither Orthodox Judaism nor the Christian faith specifies the origin of divine creation, although Christianity generally speculates that they are eternal beings created at some point in "eternity past," perhaps long before humanity's appearance on earth.[232]

The Jinn are evil and conniving beings created two thousand years before humanity and have the power to materialize at any time of their choosing and can die as human beings.[233] Extrabiblical literature from the Jewish and Christian religions have Angelic stories describing their hierarchies, creations, and downfalls that overlap with the current Islamic angelology but veer off from the chronological placement of these occurrences.[234] Indeed, the origins of these beliefs outlined above do not corroborate narratives biblically about the emergence of angelic creation, so their roots, as shown above, lie in some distorted Judaic or sectarian Christian cults in the AP

---

[230] Bialik et al., *The Book of Legends.* 12:44–5; 13:46–9, 12–3, 15 n3.

[231] Safiur-Rahman and Al-Mubarakpuri, *Tafsir Ibn Kathir. Vol. 10*, 193–203. Safiur-Rahman and Al-Mubarakpuri, *Tafsir Ibn Kathir. Vol. 5*, 391–5. Vivian A. Laughlin, *A Brief Overview of Al-Jinn within Islamic Cosmology and Religiosity.* Retrieved from: https://digitalcommons.andrews.edu/cgi/viewcontent.cgi?article=1268&context=jams#:~:text=It%20is%20said%20that%20the%20jinn%20were%20on,that%20the%20jinn%20were%20the%20first%20creatures%20created.

[232] Pearlman, *Teologia Biblica y Sistematica*, 58.

[233] Za'i et al., *Sahih Muslim Vol. 7. Hadith [6899] 67-(2717)*, 92. Bukhari shows Jinn arguing with each other about Muhammad's message and some repenting. Bukhari shows that the Jinn lived before humans appeared and drove them with madness. Khan, *Sahih Al-Bukhari Vol. 6. Hadith 4921*, 370–1. Dakdok shows Jinn appeared two thousand years before man. Dakdok, *Exposing the Truth About the Qur'an. Vol. 2 of 2*, 322.

[234] Lockman, *Gen. 6:1–4; Isa. 6:2; 14:12–5; Eze. 28:12–6; Dan. 10:13, 21; 12:1; 2 Pet. 4, 10–1; Jude. 1:6–8, 16–7, Rev. 12:4, 7–9*, 1147, 1160, 1385–6, 1444, 1447, 2212–3, 2236, 2260. Second Temple Judaic writings from the second century BC affirm this researcher's observation. Heiser, *Reversing Hermon*, 7–30, 50–2, 193–6.

and ancient pagan Arab tales.[235] Thus, after reviewing these passages above concerning the Jinn, Kaaba, black stone, and Hajj, one must consider whether Islam authentically identifies as an Abrahamic faith.

---

[235] The Arabic version says "Arabs" used to worship Jinn instead of "Mankind." Khan, *Sahih Al-Bukhari Vol. 6. Hadith 4714*, 191–2. Peterson suggests that the Jinn are part of Arabic folklore, predating Islam (pg. 93). Peterson, Mark Allen. "From Jinn to Genies." *Folklore/Cinema: Popular Film as Vernacular Culture* 1 (2007): 93. Retrieved from: https://www.researchgate.net/profile/Sharon-Sherman/publication/37721479_FolkloreCinema_Popular_Film_as_Vernacular_Culture/links/544a90c80cf2bcc9b1 d2f668/Folklore-Cinema-Popular-Film-as-Vernacular-Culture.pdf#page=101.

Discussion

After assessing the origins of Islam according to all the information provided above, the Islamic religion tends to show signs that it never initially emerged as a purely new and unified Arabic theology because it overlapped with many Jewish and Christian elements, which appear somewhat conceptually distorted. Moreover, this thesis stated earlier that although one can advocate for the position of historical momentum regarding the existence of the Meccan individual Qathem from the Quraysh tribe using the Christ title "Muhammad" to perform exploits on behalf of the Arabization of the AP, he remains a dubious figure. Nevertheless, the unchallenged imperialism that conquered many Western and Eastern Christian territories and the Persian Empire by unifying the Arab peoples under the banner of Islam remains an undeniable historical reality. This writer believes that for the religious, political, and ethnic unification of the Arab peoples who did not all consider themselves as such to occur, a charismatic figure, whether under the seventh- and eighth-century Umayyad and Abbasid caliphates or earlier than the seventh-century warlord Islam acknowledges today as its prophet, Muhammad existed.[236] People follow leaders with influence over localities more than established governments, which seems more convincing considering that the Syrian governor Mu'awiya counted on a body of preexistent Islamic believers who had already enslaved fellow Arab Jews and Christians to serve the caliphate.[237]

---

[236] Goldschmidt Jr. and Boum, *A Concise History of the Middle East*, 55, 60, 66.
[237] Ibid., 52–3.

However, believing that the full development of the Islamic faith's fame, influence, and power (in that order) did not occur until the late seventh or early eighth century AD does not pose a historical problem considering that much of its message was quite like the oppositional anti-Trinitarian Christianity developed three centuries earlier.[238] As stated earlier, John Damascene was not far from an accurate assessment when he considered the developing Islamic doctrine Christologically heretical like Monophysitism and called it an Ishmaelite heresy.[239] Although Ohlig suggests that Damascene erroneously said Ismaelites worshiped a stone, perhaps referring to some Christological inscription on a rock like that of Al-Aqsa mosque, as a Syro-Arab Christian, who's to say that it did not refer to the ongoing religious developments of an Islamized Arabized monotheism under a faith leader? Muslims today still walk around the Kaaba and, when the opportunity arises, kiss the black stone as its alleged prophet explicitly demonstrated despite this ritualistic practice's origins coming from the ancient paganism of the AP. Although it appears that the Meccan Kaaba for an extended period contained images of Jesus Christ and the Virgin Mary, insinuating its use as an ancient Christian church, Arab pagans and Muslims definitively returned it to its paganized origins by performing the same type of rituals despite the variant symbolic meanings for the latter two groups.[240]

After all, Ohlig states that Abd al-Malik most likely followed a uniquely Arabized Christianity that no longer used the imagery of the Cross on his coins. This implicated the Messianic figure no longer referring to Jesus Christ because Arabized monotheism adopted other unbiblical practices and beliefs.[241] Thus, Christianity may have played a significant role in Islam's origins but lost its influence as it continued to develop. However, the Arabization of Islam's initial

---

[238] Karl-Heinz Ohlig, *Early Islam: A Critical Reconstruction Based on Contemporary Sources* (Amherst, NY: Prometheus Books, 2014), 260–1

[239] Ibid., 270–1. Andrew Louth, *St. John Damascene, and Tradition. Pg. 7*. Received from: https://oxford-universitypressscholarship-com.ezproxy.liberty.edu/view/1 0.1093/0199252386.001.0001/acprof-9780199252381-chapter-2?print=pdf.

[240] Guillaume, *The Life of Muhammad*, 552.

[241] Ohlig, *Early Islam,* 263.

non-Trinitarian Christian faith shaped its monotheistic notions by negating its Abrahamic predecessors' more significant theological contributions by inherently distorting their doctrinal beliefs.

Another noticeable issue when attempting to reform Islamic beliefs by reinterpreting its Arabic script through a Syro-Aramaic reading is that it does not eliminate the historical outcome created by its initial followers' ancient socioreligious ideologies propelling its conquest of the Middle East by imposing their beliefs. After all, Islam's origin did not solely rely on Judaism and Christianity's theological contributions. Many Arab peoples were Jews and Christians throughout the previous centuries during the very inceptions of these religions in the AP, specifically Mecca.[242] Lüling's third thesis shows that despite the oldest non-Trinitarian form of Arabic Christianity's influence in the AP's Central region, the birth of the Islamic religion comes from a reversion to the tribalistic cultural traditions of the Arabs.[243]

One may immediately assume that the theological reversal above implies returning to the monotheistic Abrahamic faith of the Jews and Arabs, denying the deification of *Yeshua HaMashiach.* However, on a sour note, regression to the Arabic tribalistic tradition meant that Qathem, or the individual acting under the Christ title Muhammad, incorporated violence to impose his alleged Hanifdom on all he encountered in his lifetime, as the *hanif,* Abu Amir of Aus pointed out.[244] Abu Amir rejected Muhammad's claim to be a *hanif.*

Indeed, these observations mentioned above by Abu Amir of Aus were not Judaic or Christian but exclusively Arab tribalism, leading to the 1,400-year early development and modern-day establish-

---

[242] Guillaume, *The Life of Muhammad,* 11–7, 271. Webb, *Imagining the Arabs,* 80–1.

[243] Lüling, *A Challenge to Islam for Reformation,* 20–22.

[244] Ibid., 358–9. Macintosh-Smith shows the cruel raiding practices of the Arabic peoples. Macintosh-Smith, *Arabs,* 58–9, 61–3. Muhammad continued the tribal practices of raiding, pillaging, and humiliating unbelievers, mandated in the chapter of Al-Tawba. Dakdok, *The Generous Qur'an. Surah.* 8:67–9; 9:28–9, 110, 114.

ment of Sunni and Shi'a Islam.[245] One cannot judge a religion by the behaviors of its adherents but by the alleged sayings of its gods in its sacred writings, which contextually suggest that if Islam began under Jewish and Christian theologies, it became violent early on, making itself a pariah to the moral principles of the Abrahamic faiths. The Qur'an contains many non-Trinitarian Christian hymnodies within its pages because of the Syro-Aramaic used by many Arabic-speaking Christians at the time of its emergence.[246] Still, the reality remains that numerous passages exist speaking against the divinity of Jesus Christ, misrepresenting Trinitarian concepts, and ultimately commanding all Muslim believers to physically persecute Jews, Christians, and unbelievers for all time (e.g., surah 9:29, 73, 123). If one justifies these passages as later additions done by the Umayyad to unify Arabized Christianity, it still needed an ideologically traditional basis for its successful acceptance in the religious community that famously applied its religiously politicized military structure recognized early in its development until today. This researcher argues that the problem does not wholly rest with the Arab people who were faithful Jews and Christians but with the impact of a charismatic leader(s) who gained vital followers to compel their conformity to his religious ideologies by military measures.

This thesis indicates that the creation of the Qur'an by necessity comes from the intent to unify the Arab people under one religion that many could accept as authentic because it is no mystery that many Arabs knew about their filial lineage and monotheistic connection to the Judaeo-Christian God (see footnote 60, 65–66). However, to suggest that Qathem, the user of the Christ title Muhammad, continued in the monotheistic traditions of his Jewish cousins or even the Arab Christians he warred against remains a fallacy that many well-intentioned Westerners tend to believe by wishing he identified as an alleged *hanif.* The proof of the observation above comes from the Qur'an's supposed compilation, badly plagiarized chronol-

---

[245] Momen explains the Sunni and Shi'I split due to infighting in this newly founded religious movement. Momen, *Shi'i Islam,* 15–22.

[246] Luxenberg, *The Syro-Aramaic Reading of the Koran,* 10–11, 70–1. Warraq, *What the Koran Really Says,* 82–3.

ogies, and garbled monotheistic theology, which justifies in one way or another the ulterior reasons for so many diverse scholarly opinions about its creation. For example, Youssif states that Muhammad had minimal knowledge of the biblical scriptures used by Jews and Christians, which leads scholars like Webb and Spencer, after examination, to posit that because organized Islamic literature appeared two centuries later, perhaps Muhammad never existed.[247] Thus, it seems that much of the Qur'an remains a book filled with distorted biblical stories, strange Christological hymnodies, and an array of virulent mandates affirmed by ahadith compilations Arabizing the identity of its alleged prophet and peoples validating its narratives against unbelievers.[248]

The most intriguing observation surrounding the religious origins of Islam points to the ulterior reasoning behind the inclusion of so much Christological and theological content attempting to affirm its authority over its predecessors while claiming Abrahamic legitimacy. This thesis shows that much effort has highlighted the title used for God in Judaism, Christianity, and Islam may etymologically identify the same deity (i.e., El, Eloah, and Allah). Still, this writer believes that a closer examination of the moral and existential character traits shows that the Islamic Allah remains wholly distinct. Moreover, the origins of the Judaic and Christian God remain validated by experiential accounts between Him and Israel, recorded by the Jewish prophets, and ultimately, through the appearance of the deific figure of Jesus Christ. According to the Christian faith, God entered His creation by living among humanity, dying for them, and finally resurrecting with all power and glory, which the Gospels,

---

[247] Youssif, *Islam in Christ's Eyes*, 48, 50–1. Webb, *Imagining the Arabs*, 151, 156, 177. See footnote 88: Warraq, *What the Koran Really Says*, 133.

[248] See Dakdok's two bound volumes on the quranic version of the biblical narratives about the Jewish prophets, which will show either Muhammad's or the later writers of the Qur'an and ahadith compilations' utter confusion twisting the Bible's theological and historical content. Dakdok, *Exposing the Truth About the Qur'an. Vol. 1 and 2.* Moreover, see the entirety of the works of Luxenberg, Lüling, Webb, Maalouf, and Spencer and all the scholars mentioned in this thesis.

the Pauline and Johannine epistles, and other epistolary writers recorded.[249]

Unquestionably, the ancient Hebrew and early Jewish Christians' historical accounts of their interactions with their God remain much more reliable than any Islamic source because of the mere proximity between the writers to the events. Licona demonstrates this fact by corroborating the Christian historical accounts of Jesus Christ with the writings of secular writers that incidentally mention biblical personalities and events while addressing the significant issues of their time. For example, Licona shows the works of non-Christians like Josephus, Suetonius, Mara bar Serapion, Tacitus, Thallus, Julius Africanus, and Lucian.[250] Josephus maintained the unique position of knowing the priests of Jesus's day and most likely heard Jesus and the Apostles preach at some point.[251] Furthermore, Julius Africanus mentions Thallus's testimony of the strange meteorological and geological phenomena that occurred during the crucifixion of Jesus Christ, confirming the Synoptic Gospels' accounts.[252] Indeed, postmodernists' rejection of the miraculous does not detract from the truth of the historical event affirmed by eyewitnesses considered firsthand sources and the secondhand informants who recorded the historical accounts after hearing them, which most likely experienced the divine power behind their words.

On the other hand, despite the validation efforts of its respected Islamic scholars like Al-Qurtubi, Ibn Kathir, Al-Jalalayn, and Al-Bukhari, much of Islam came centuries later to allegedly record what they never witnessed or heard from the alleged prophet. Even the explanations of Ibn Abbas, the cousin of the prophet Muhammad, appear written too many years later to rely on his supposed experience validating qur'anic ayat confidently. It seems no

---

[249] Lockman, *Matt. 1–2, 27–8; Mk. 1, 15–16; Lk. 2, 23:44–56; 24; Jn. 1, 6–7, 11, 18–21; Acts. 9:1–32; Rom. 1:1–7.*

[250] Michael R. Licona, *The Resurrection of Jesus: A New Historiographical Approach* (Downers Grove, IL: IVP Academic, 2010), 235–7, 239–46.

[251] Ibid., 235–6.

[252] Ibid., 245. Lockman, *Matt. 27:45:54; Mk. 15:33–40; Lk. 23:44–9,* 1659, 1720, 1804.

wonder why so many doubt the existence of Muhammad and assert that Islam emerged much later than the seventh century during the rise of the Umayyad and Abbasid caliphates to create a unified distorted Arabic version of the Judaic and Christian monotheistic traditions, simultaneously demonizing them. The Arab people are special before God and always had a place with their Jewish brethren according to *Yahweh-Elohim's* promises, as seen in Maalouf's discussion of the blessings accorded to Ismael, afforded to Keturah's heritage as Abraham's wife after Sarah's death, and the Arab tribes.[253] However, as Maalouf pointed out earlier, the Arab peoples fell into idolatry early on, which somewhat appears to dismiss the narrative of the hanifiyyan report about pure Islamic monotheistic worship of Allah in the Meccan province. The actual monotheists in the Arab regions were not the Islamic creation of an Arabized hanifiyyan community but the Syriac, Aramean, and Arab Jews and Christians who resided in the AP.[254]

Lastly, no authentic justification for Islamic practices considered mandatory and holy like the pilgrimage to Mecca to perform Hajj and the rituals accompanying its completion, clearly originating from Arab paganism, fit into any Jewish or Christian practices. Although one can point to Judaism's legalistic ritual requirements and the ancient pilgrimages of Christians to Jerusalem, which both groups considered holy, no biblical mandates for the pagan practices or beliefs of Islam exist, except the sinful rituals of the ANE religions and Hellenistic idolatry. As shown earlier, the Jewish mythologies Islam adhered to for some doctrinal requirements distinguish themselves from orthodox Judaic beliefs (see section above on God and the Angelic beings). Moreover, the Arabic Christian sectarian influence on Islam's monotheistic faith differs from its Islamic divine commands of forcing their Allah on others by any means necessary and does not biblically fit any doctrine in Western or Eastern orthodox Christianity. Therefore, despite the Jewish and Christian theological contributions to Islam, its origins remain an artificially Arabized ver-

---

[253] Maalouf, *Arabs in the Shadow of Israel*, 132–5, 144–5, 184–5, 206.
[254] Webb, *Imagining the Arabs*, 79–81, 95, 115–6, 261–9.

sion of the Abrahamic faiths, which developed its religious ideology on tribalistic tendencies that include abhorrent paganistic elements many Arab Christians reject.

Conclusion

Overall, Islam's founding and religious practices are enabled by the writings of the Qur'an, ahadith, and the tafsirs, which the majority consider sacred and the lynchpin connecting them to Allah through their submission and obedience to their prophet Muhammad. Although the ahadith giving the qur'anic surahs its context began to emerge nearly two hundred years later than when the alleged prophet lived in Mecca, faithful Muslims believe that these writings are the sunnah (sayings) of Muhammad. Many Muslims do not always reflect on or dare ask questions about the origins of their prophet, writings, scholars, or their deity Allah to keep in line with Muhammad's command (e.g., Qur'an 5:101). Unlike the Judaeo-Christian God, who invites His worshipers to reason with Him (e.g., Isaiah 1:17, 41:21), Allah does not welcome such inquiries, at least according to his prophet Muhammad. However, one notices that Muslims living in the West have become more Westernized and have willingly exposed themselves to the Judaeo-Christian custom of their brethren mentioned above. Muslims have begun questioning the origins of Islamic practices concerning Allah by parsing the sunnah and deeds of their prophet Muhammad (i.e., Nabeel Qureshi, the Caner brothers, Ayaan Hirsi Ali, Zhudi Jasser, and Majid Nawaz).

Islam does not define the Arabic people because they existed long before its emergence. After its sociopolitical rise, Jewish, Christian, and pagan Arabs lived throughout the AP and continue to exist worldwide under all these religious categories and even as atheists. Arabic history remains incredibly rich, as may be observed throughout this thesis by examining their genealogical origins, ancient contributions, and religious diversity before the arrival of Islam. Once

Islam arrived on the world stage, most Arab peoples were unified under one sociopolitical movement with aggressive tendencies against its Abrahamic predecessors and coreligionists. However, this matter mentioned above causes one to notice Islam's moral and theological deviation from Judaism and Christianity, leading scholars to investigate the personal character, religious beliefs, and history of the mysterious Islamic figure acknowledged by all Muslims worldwide as Muhammad, Allah's alleged prophet. As seen in the body of this thesis, Muhammad's existence remains a dubious issue because the appearance of his inspirations, the Qur'an and ahadith compilations two centuries later, causes scholars to suspect that leaders motived to unify the Arabian Peninsula had a hand in the process.

After all, the reality that tribalism played a significant role throughout the history of the Arabian Peninsula, and those considered Arabs today did not view themselves as Arabs, nor did they share the same gods, causes one to consider the possibility of social engineering enacted during the time of the caliphates. Despite the valid opinions of many of the brilliant scholars cited throughout this thesis, this author argues that the Christ title Muhammad was usurped by an actual person that existed and convinced many to speak and act under the divine authority of Allah, the primary deity of the ancient Arabs. However, the doubt that assails this writer's conscience is whether the ministry of Qathem occurred in Mecca. After closely scrutinizing the significance of Mecca during the period of Qathem's alleged prophetic ministry, the location did not seem significant enough considering the historical trading and religious importance of the Nabataean and Southern Arabian kingdoms that still traded with Western and Eastern empires. Moreover, the geographical depictions in some of the passages of the Qur'an, ahadith, and the sira of Muhammad become even more troublesome for the location of Mecca as the primary trading depot of the ancient Middle Eastern world.

The Judaic and Christian presence in the Arabian Peninsula before Islam influenced the religion's monotheistic character. However, by taking a closer look at the doctrinal founding of the Islamic faith, one can observe that Judaism and sectarian Christianity had the most profound effect on its monotheistic views, angelology, and legalisms shaping its aggressivity against orthodox Arab Jews and Trinitarian Christians. The beliefs mentioned above regarding angels paralleled Jewish mythology and Christian sectarians over traditional Judaism and Christianity. Moreover, Arab tribalistic paganism was incorporated into Islam. However, parts of the rituals were restructured to honor Allah as the only true deity of the AP. Nevertheless, the violent characteristics of the Islamic faith against all unbelievers and the people of the book veer off from its Abrahamic predecessors significantly because its scriptures mandate their absolute subjugation and humiliation, which resemble the tribalistic behaviors depicted in ancient Arabic poetry.

Finally, although Islamic scholars suggest that the Qur'an remains purely Arabic writing, nothing could be further from the truth of that statement. The Qur'an has many foreign words of Syriac and Aramean origin, which has caused numerous scholars to study its script more closely, which led to the discovery that some of its passages contain Christological hymnodies that triggered an immediate inquiry into whether all its texts were initially Islamic. According to Luxenberg, Lüling, Warraq, and Spencer, many of the Qur'an's passages glorify Jesus Christ. He is the rightful possessor of the title Muhammad if one rereads its texts under a Syro-Aramaic "linguistic lens." This author believes without a shadow of a doubt that many passages of the Qur'an were added much later to resemble the Islamic theology today despite maintaining Christological texts within its pages.

The origins of Islam's founder and religious practices remain somewhat muddled and need further investigation, but Islam does carry an Arabized monotheistic character. Nonetheless, the biblical God has blessed the Arabic peoples from the beginning of their existence. God has a restorative plan to enact His salvation on their behalf to break free from the Abrahamic Judaeo-Christian cult of Islam.

Bibliography

Al-Fassi, Hatoon Ajwad. *Women in Pre-Islamic Arabia: Nabataea.* Oxford, UK: Bar Publishing, 2016.

Al-Hilali, Muhammad Taqi-ud-Din, and Muhammad Khan. *Interpretations of The Meanings of The Noble Qur'an in The English Language: A Summarized Version of At-Tabari, Al-Qurtubi, and Ibn Kathir with Comments from Sahih Al-Bukhari. Vol. 1.* Riyadh, Saudi: Darussalam, 1996.

Ali, Ayaan Hirsi. *Prey: Immigration, Islam, and the Erosion of Women's Rights.* New York, NY: Harper-Collins, 2021.

Al-Mubarakpuri, Safiur-Rahman. *Tafsir Ibn Kathir: Surat Al-Jathiya to the end of Surat Al-Muunafiqun. Abridged. Vol. 9.* Brooklyn, NY: Darussalam, 2003.

__________ *Tafsir Ibn Kathir: Surat Al-Isra', Verse 39 to the end of Surat Al-Mu'minun. Abridged. Vol. 6.* Brooklyn, NY: Darussalam, 2003.

__________. *Tafsir Ibn Kathir: Surat Al-Baqarah, Verse 253 to Surat An-Nisa, Verse 147. to the end of Surat Al-Muunafiqun. Abridged. Vol. 2.* Brooklyn, NY: Darussalam, 2003.

__________. *Tafsir Ibn Kathir: Surat Al-A'raf, to the end of Surat Yunus. Abridged. Vol. 4.* Brooklyn, NY: Darussalam, 2003.

__________. *Tafsir Ibn Kathir: Surat Al-Jathiya to the end of Surat Al-Muunafiqun. Abridged. Vol. 10.* Brooklyn, NY: Darussalam, 2003.

Bauckham, Richard. *Jesus and the God of Israel: God Crucified and Other Studies on the New Testament's Christology of Divine Identity.* Grand Rapids, MI: Eerdmans Publishing, 2009.

Bewley, Aisha, Bewley, Abdalhaqq, and Waley, Muhammad Isa. *Tafsir Al-Jalalayn*. London, UK: Dar Al Taqwa Ltd., 2014.

Bialik, Hayim Nahman, Ravnitzky, Yehoshua Hana, Braude, William G., Stern, David. *The Book of Legends Sefer Ha-Aggadah: Legends from the Talmud and Midrash*. New York, NY: Schocken Books, 1992.

Block, Daniel. *The Gods of the Nations: A Study in Ancient Near Eastern National Theology. 2nd Ed.* Eugene, OR: Wipf and Stock Publishers, 2000.

________. *Israel: Ancient Kingdom or Late Invention?* Nashville, TN: B&H Academic, 2008.

Brown, Raymond E. *An Introduction to the New Testament.* New Haven, CT: Yale Aybrl, 2010.

Caner, Ergun Mehmet and Caner, Emir Fethi. *Unveiling Islam: An Insider's look at Muslim Life and Beliefs. Updated and Expanded Edition.* Grand Rapids, MI: Kregel Publications, 2009.

Carroll, Michael P. *The Cult of the Virgin Mary: Psychological Origins.* Princeton, NJ: Princeton University Press, 1986.

Carvalho, Corrine L. *Encountering Ancient Voices: A Guide to Reading the Old Testament. 2nd Ed.* Winona, MN: Anselm Academic, 2010.

Torrey, Charles C. "A New Era in the History of the 'Apocrypha.'" *The Monist* 25, no. 2 (1 April 1915): 286–294. https://doi.org/10.5840/monist191525211.

Corduan, Winfried. *Neighboring Faiths: A Christian Introduction to World Religions. Second Edition.* Downers Grove, IL: IVP Academic, 2012.

Cory, Catherine. *A Voyage Through the New Testament. Custom Edition for Saint Leo University. REL. 110.* Upper Saddle River, NJ: Pearson, 2008.

Dakdok, Usama K. *Exposing the Truth about the Qur'an: The Revelation of the Error. The Story of the Prophets. Vol. 1 of 2.* Venice, FL: Usama Dakdok Publishing, 2013.

________. *Exposing the Truth About the Qur'an: The Revelation of Error. The Stories of the Prophets. Vol. 2 of 2.* Venice, FL: Usama Dakdok Publishing, 2013.

__________. *The Generous Qur'an: An Accurate English Translation.* Venice, FL: Usama Dakdok, 2015.

Dulles, Avery Cardinal. *A History of Apologetics.* San Francisco, CA: Ignatius Press, 2005.

Fernandez-Morera, Dario. *The Myth of the Andalusian Paradise: Muslims, Christians, and Jews Under Islamic Rule in Medieval Spain.* Wilmington, DE: ISI Books, 2016.

Gibson, Dan. *The Nabataeans: Builders of Petra.* Orlando, FL: Xlibris, 2022.

Goldschmidt, Arthur, and Boum, Aomar. *A Concise History of the Middle East. 11th Ed.* Boulder, CO: Westview Press, 2016.

Green Sr., Jay P. *The Interlinear Bible: Hebrew, Greek, and English with Strong's Concordance Numbers Above Each Word. Genesis. 10:8-11; 11:1-9.* Peabody, MA: Hendrickson Publishers, 2008.

Groothuis, Douglass. *Christian Apologetics: A Comprehensive Case for Biblical Faith.* Downers Grove, IL: IVP Academic, 2011.

Guillaume, Alfred. *The Life of Muhammad: A Translation of Ishaq's Sirat Rasul Allah.* Karachi, PAK: Oxford University Press, 2016.

Heiser, Michael S. *Reversing Hermon: Enoch, the Watchers, and the Forgotten Mission of Jesus Christ.* Crane, MO: Defender Publishing, 2017.

Kaiser Jr., Walter C., and Moises Silva. *Introduction to Biblical Hermeneutics: The Search for Meaning. Revised and Expanded Edition.* Grand Rapids, MI: Zondervan, 2011.

Karim, Adnan, and Ayman Khalid. *Secrets Within the Order of the Qur'an: al-Hafiz, al-Mufassir. Jalal al-Din al-Suyuti (d. 911h).* Birmingham, UK: Dar al-Arqam Publishing, 2018.

Khan, Muhammad Muhsin. *The Translation of the Meanings of Sahih Al-Bukhari. Arabic-English. Vol. 1. Ahadith 001 to 875. hadith 344.* Riyadh, SAE: Darussalam, 2008.

__________. *The Translation of the Meanings of Sahih Al-Bukhari. Arabic-English. Vol. 5. 3649 to 4473.* Riyadh, SAE: Darussalam, 2008.

__________. *The Translation of the Meanings of Sahih Al-Bukhari. Arabic-English. Vol. 6. Ahadith 4474 to 5062.* Riyadh, SAE: Darussalam, 2008.

_________. *The Translation of The Meanings of Sahih Al-Bukhari. Arabic to English. Vol. 2. 876 to 1772*. Riyadh, SA: Darussalam, 2008.

_________. *The Translation of The Meanings of Sahih Al-Bukhari. Arabic to English. Vol. 4. Ahadith 2738 to 3648*. Riyadh, SUA: Darussalam, 2008.

_________. *The Translation of The Meanings of Sahih Al-Bukhari. Arabic to English. Vol. 9. Ahadith 6861 to 7563*. Riyadh, SUA: Darussalam, 2008.

Klein, William W., Craig L. Blomberg, and Robert L. Hubbard. *Introduction to Biblical Interpretation. 3rd Ed.* Grand Rapids, MI: Zondervan, 2017.

Köstenberger, Andreas J., Darrell L. Bock, and Josh Chatraw. *Truth in a Culture of Doubt: Engaging Skeptical Challenges to the Bible.* Nashville, TN: B&H Publishing Group, 2014.

Licona, Michael R. *The Resurrection of Jesus: A New Historiographical Approach.* Downers Grove, IL: IVP Academic, 2010.

Lindstedt, Ilkka Juhani. "Pre-Islamic Arabia and Early Islam." *Routledge handbook on early Islam* (2018). Retrieved from: https:// helda.helsinki.fi/bitstream/handle/10138/307521/Lindstedt_Early_Muslims_Pre_Is lamic_Arabia_and_Pagans_.pdf?sequence=1.

Lockman Foundation. *Life Application Bible Study Bible. NASB.* Grand Rapids, MI: Zondervan, 2000.

Louth, Andrew. *St. John Damascene, and Tradition. Pg. 7.* Received from: https://oxford-universitypressscholarship-com.ezproxy.liberty.edu/view/10.1093/0199252386.001.0001/acprof-9780199252381-chapter-2?print=pdf.

Luibheid, Colm et al. *Pseudo-Dionysius: The Complete Works.* Mahwah, NJ: Paulist Press, 1987.

Lüling, Günter. *A Challenge to Islam for Reformation: The Rediscovery and Reliable Reconstruction of a Comprehensive Pre-Islamic Christian Hymnal Hidden in the Koran Under Earliest Islamic Reinterpretations.* Delhi, IN: Motilal Banarsidass Publishers, 2003.

Luxenberg, Christoph [pseud]. *The Syro-Aramaic Reading of the Koran: A Contribution to the Decoding of the Language of the Koran.* Berlin, DEU: Schiler, 2007.

Maalouf, Tony. *Arabs in the Shadow of Israel: The Unfolding of God's Prophetic Plan for Ishmael's Line.* Grand Rapids, MI: Kregel Publications, 2003.

Macintosh-Smith, Tim. *Arabs: A 3,000-Year History of Peoples, Tribes, and Empires.* New Haven, CT: Yale University Press, 2019.

Mark, Joshua J. "Kingdom of Saba." *World History Encyclopedia.* Last modified March 02, 2018. https://www.worldhistory.org/Kingdom_of_Saba/.

McAuliffe, Jane Dammen. *Encyclopedia of the Qur'ān.* Vol. 6. Leiden: Brill, 2001. Retrieved from: https://scholar.google.ca/scholar?hl=en&as_sdt=0%2C10&q=ancient+pre-islamic+Sabean+Pantheon&btnG=.

Momen, Moojan. *An Introduction to Shi'i Islam.* New Haven, CT: Yale University Press, 1985.

Ohlig, Karl-Heinz. *Early Islam: A Critical Reconstruction Based on Contemporary Sources.* Amherst, NY: Prometheus Books, 2014.

Packer, J. I., Merril C. Tenney, and William White Jr. *Enciclopedia Ilustrada de Realidades de la Biblia: Una Completa Fuente de Datos Sobre Personas, Lugares, y Costumbres de la Biblia. [Original title: Nelson's Illustrated Encyclopedia of Bible Facts.* Thomas Nelson Publishers, 1980]. Miami, FL: Caribe, 2002.

Pearlman, Myer. *Teologia Biblica y Sistematica. [English Version, Knowing the Doctrines of the Bible].* Miami, FL: Editorial Vida, 1992.

Peterson, Mark Allen. "From Jinn to Genies." *Folklore/Cinema: Popular Film as Vernacular Culture* 1 (2007): 93. Retrieved from: https://www.researchgate.net/profile/Sharon-Sherman/publication/37721479_FolkloreCinema_Popular_Film_as_Vernacular_Culture/links/544a90c80cf2bcc9b1d2f668/Folklore-Cinema-Popular-Film-as-Vernacular-Culture.pdf#page=101.

Pinch, Geraldine. *Egyptian Mythology: A Guide to the Gods, Goddesses, and Traditions of Ancient Egypt.* New York, NY: Oxford University Press, 2004.

Prince, Christian [pseud]. *El Engaño de Allah (English version, The Deception of Allah)*. Columbia, SC: Christian Prince, 2019.

__________. *Sex & Allah. Vol. I.* Columbia, SC: Christian Prince, 2018.

__________. *Sex & Allah. Vol. 2.* Columbia, SC: Christian Prince, 2018.

Roark, Dallas M. *Answering Islam: A Christian-Muslim Dialogue. Is There Jihad in the Old Testament?* Retrieved from: https://answering-islam.org/authors/roark/jihad_ot.html.

Shamoun, Sam. *Answering Islam: Revisiting the Identity of the Pre-Islamic Allah at Mecca Pt. 1. Pg. 10-4.* Retrieved from*: Sam Shamoun, Answering Islam: Revisiting the Identity of the Pre-Islamic Allah at Mecca Pt. 1. Pg. 10-4.* Retrieved from: https://answering-islam.org/authors/shamoun/preislamic_allah1.html.

Spencer, Robert. *Did Muhammad Exist? An Inquiry into Islam's Obscure Origins. Revised and Expanded Edition.* New York, NY: Bombardier, 2021.

__________The Critical Qur'an: Explained from Key Commentaries and Contemporary Historical Research. New York, NY: Bombardier, 2021.

US Department of State. *2019 Report on International Religious Freedom: Jordan. Office of International Religious Freedom.* Retrieved from: https://www.state.gov/reports/2019-report-on-international-religious-freedom/jordan/?msclkid=48856c12ac6c11e-cb7745008b0739c95.

Valkenberg, Pim. *World Religions in Dialogue: A Comparative Theological Approach.* Winona, MN: Anselm Academic, 2013.

Warner, Bill. *Sharia for Non-Muslims: Center for the Study of Political Islam. ISBN 0-97957948-1 and ISBN 978-0-9795794-8-6. V I.23.2017.* (USA, CSPI, LLC, 2010), 25. Retrieved from: https://petterssonsblogg.se/wp-content/uploads/2017/05/sharia_law_for_non-muslims.pdf.

Warraq, Ibn. *What the Koran Really Says: Language, Text, and Commentary.* Amherst, NY: Prometheus Books, 2002.

Webb, Peter. *Imagining the Arabs: Arab Identity and the Rise of Islam.* Edinburgh, UK: Edinburgh University Press, 2016.

Yathrib Islamic Archaeology Glossary 2007 Joukowsky Institute for Archaeology & the Ancient World. *Brown University. Posted at Oct 14/2007 05:56 PM.* Retrieved from: https://brown.edu/Departments/Joukowsky_Institute/courses/islamicarchaeologyglossary 2007/4083.html

Youssif, Wissam. *Islam in Christ's Eyes: A Scriptural Study on the Origins of Islam and the Christian Response.* Middletown, DE: ACM, 2021.

Za'i, Hafiz Abu Tahir Zubair. "Ali, Al-Khattab, Nasiruddin, and Khaliyl, Abu. *English Translation of Sahih Muslim Compiled by: Imam Abul Hussain Muslim Ibn al-Hajjaj. Vol. 2.* Brooklyn, NY: Darussalam, 2007.

__________. *English Translation of Sahih Muslim Compiled by: Imam Abul Hussain Muslim Ibn al-Hajjaj. Vol. 1.* Brooklyn, NY: Darussalam, 2007.

__________. *English Translation of Sahih Muslim Compiled by: Imam Abul Hussain Muslim Ibn al-Hajjaj. Vol. 7.* Brooklyn, NY: Darussalam, 2007.

__________. *English Translation of Sahih Muslim. Vol. 6. From Hadith no. 5646 to 6722.* Brooklyn, NY: Darussalam, 2007.

Acknowledgments

I would like to thank so many friends, colleagues, and family members who have contributed to encouraging my desire of reaching the multitudes of religious people in the surrounding community and the larger audience of Western academia worldwide with a clear, concise depiction of this Christian's perspective on Islam. Still, I want to acknowledge the extraordinary efforts and support of my sister who believed that my views and work in the theological field should be publicized for the good of many Christians who believe Islam stands as an extension of the Abrahamic faith. Moreover, I thank my children for their loving support and faith in my ability to teach such topics with the underlying goal of reaching young Christians like themselves, and many Western Muslims who simply seek the truth about God wherever it resides. Above all, I want to thank our Heavenly Father for my Lord and Savior Jesus Christ who graciously equipped me through His Holy Spirit to carry forth his word and this investigative work to reach the minds and hearts of Jews, Christians, Muslims, and all religious believers and secular students seeking to understand Islam.

A Word about the Author (ATA)

Gabriel Aryeh is originally from the Bronx, New York. During his teen years, Aryeh became a Christian by the divine grace and intention of the Triune God recognized by believers professing the authentic Christian faith. As a youth raised in the Bronx during the 1970s and 1980s, Aryeh's parents were loving, hardworking individuals who attempted to raise him with the best ethical standards their societal and cultural traditions offered. However, the many prayers, biblical teachings, and guidance of his grandmother who consistently encouraged him to attend Sunday school and Friday services in an old-time evangelical church near Crotona Park (the Bronx) deserve much credit for Aryeh's obedience to God's call into the Christian faith and service. After fourteen years of faithful ministerial service in a Bronx church, Aryeh served in lead and associate pastoral positions throughout various states and attained a BA in religion, psychology, and a ThM in Christian apologetics. Moreover, Aryeh has written several unpublished papers on theological topics showing their historical verifications, philosophical coherence, and theoretical competence.

Today, Aryeh continues to write and comment on several topics involving political matters, which have ultimately led to theological discussions involving the theoretical premise of societal matters affecting modern Western civilization and its quotidian lifestyle. As a strong believer that the West remains founded upon Judaeo-Christian principles, Aryeh has noticed the rise of many secular and religious ideas that have infiltrated the Christian foundations of the United States and all Western civilization. However, Aryeh observed how Islam made significant inroads into the minds of many Christian Americans within English and Spanish-speaking communities, causing some to erroneously abandon their faith in Christ. Hence, the aforementioned observation initiated the efforts to educate the American public about the nature and intention of the Islamic religion.